FINDING
THE LIGHT

THE KINGDOM OF HEAVEN AND HOW TO ENTER IT

A PERSONAL STUDY

DONALD E. JONES, PHD

J & A Book Publishers
www.jabookpublishers.com

ISBN-13: 978-0692740682
ISBN-10: 0692740686

DEDICATION

I dedicate this book to my Savior and Lord Jesus Christ. He has been with me every step of my journey upon the Earth, and I so look forward to being in His presence forever and ever.

CONTENTS

ACKNOWLEDGMENTS

I want to thank my wonderful and gracious wife Carol who has supported me in this ministry with sacrifice, enthusiasm, encouragement, and accountability. Most of all, she has been a constant blessing because of her willingness to listen. I was always sharing with her the truths God had been teaching me as I studied His word and wrote this book. It consumed many hours. Thank you, Carol and I deeply love you.

I want to thank my son Gregory R. Jones for volunteering to be the primary editor of this important book. Without his time and effort in painstakingly and meticulously going over every word and every sentence checking and rechecking the sentence structure and grammar, I would not have been able to complete it. Thank you for your ministry to me. I love you my son.

I want to thank my other children, Krista, Matt, and Kara for their love for Christ and His Word and their willingness to live for Him. I love you all.

Introduction

Years ago, as a school administrator of a middle school, I received a call that a six-year-old special needs child had left the elementary campus a quarter mile away and was on the run. Right after the call, a woman walked into the office and claimed she had been following a small child walking alone. She was afraid to stop him because somebody might think that she was kidnapping him. Now, he was standing in the middle of the junction of two streets singing aloud without realizing the danger he was in.

Suddenly, I felt myself bolt out the door and begin to run at full speed. Down two blocks I ran until I found the child. He was just standing there singing in complete naivety to the unhappy ending he was about to have. I walked slowly toward him and showed him my badge and radio to identify who I was. I explained that I was from a nearby school and wanted to help him. I grabbed his hand and walked him out of his potentially disastrous ending. I would like to do the same in a spiritual way for you. Someone did it for me.

You might now be thinking, "What potentially dangerous ending?" It is an eternity without God and His heaven. This eternity without Him and His presence is terribly dangerous because it involves everlasting punishment. An eternity with God in His heaven entails everlasting blessing. This book was written to show you the light to the path that will lead you to heaven. That "Light" is Jesus Christ. In John 14:1-4, the Lord Jesus Himself declared this, "Don't let your heart be troubled. Believe in God. Believe also in me. In my Father's house are many homes. If it weren't so, I would have told you. I am going to prepare a place [in heaven] for you. If I go and prepare a place [in heaven] for you, I will come again, and will receive you to myself; that where I am, you may be there

1

also. Where I go, you know, and you know the way." Jesus declared to them that they knew the way to heaven.

Then in John 14:5-6 Thomas, who was one of His twelve disciples, asked a question, "Thomas said to him, 'Lord, we don't know where you are going. How can we know the way?' Jesus said to him, 'I am the way, the truth, and the life. No one comes to the Father, except through me.'" Jesus is the only way to God's heaven. Now you may be thinking that you have heard all this before, but you haven't. You may have heard a few of its parts, but you have not heard the whole story. As I tell you this "whole story," I will provide some of the passages from the Bible that teach it. This is incredibly important. It is not my kingdom I am about to describe but God's kingdom. So, you must hear it in His own words, not mine. Open your mind and hold on! In John 12:46, Jesus proclaimed, "I have come as a light into the world, that whoever believes in me may not remain in the darkness."

The word "light" means truth and holiness revealed. Jesus is the embodiment of God's truth and holiness which God wanted revealed to us. In His light we will find the path to the kingdom of God's heaven. This light is the gospel of Jesus Christ. If you are willing to receive this light and decide to enter the kingdom of heaven, all the blessings of heaven are yours (Ephesian 1:3). As I share these truths with you, I will discuss experiences I have had sharing the gospel. To ensure confidentiality, I added, subtracted, changed, or invented details so no person can be identified. Yet, the experiences are real, and these people placed their faith in Jesus Christ as Savior and Lord. All found a new purpose, destiny, and real fulfillment. Some are now in heaven having escaped their dangerous fate and unhappy ending. Others are still alive living out their destiny. May the Holy Spirit work in your life as I share the good news with you.

Chapter 1

Realize our Divine Love

In *A Tale of Two Cities*, Charles Dickens wrote, "It was the best of times, it was the worst of times, it was the age of wisdom, it was the age of foolishness, it was the epoch of belief, it was the epoch of incredulity, it was the season of Light, it was the season of Darkness, it was the spring of hope, it was the winter of despair, we had everything before us, we had nothing before us, we were all going direct to heaven, we were all going direct the other way-in short, the period was so far like the present period, that some of its noisiest authorities insisted on its being received, for good or for evil, in the superlative degree of comparison only. The world is in chaos." Indeed, the world is in chaos but not as the author imagines. The world is in the chaos of unbelief.

This chaos has caused numerous problems for you and me. For every Christian, the chaos affords opportunities for wisdom, belief, light, and most of all hope in Jesus Christ. For non-Christians, it becomes a lifetime of great foolishness, incredulity, darkness, and despair not only now but in the life to come. This is you and it was me. For the problems of this life, you might speak to counselors, therapists, friends, physicians, and others for help, comfort, and even guidance. Perhaps, these people and others could give some solace with some solutions for this life, but only Christians utilizing the Word of our God (as I am right now with you) are able to provide supernatural solutions with comfort for this life and into eternity. This is the reason why I wrote this book.

One part of Dickens' statement was not true, "We were all going direct to heaven, we were all going direct the other way." Few are going direct to heaven, and many are going the other way. In Matthew 7:13-14, Jesus said that men were to enter in the narrow gate. The gate to destruction is wide and broad; but to life, it is narrow and restricted. Few enter by it. If you have not received Jesus as Savior and Lord the way the Scriptures indicate, then you are on that broad road leading to your destruction right now! You do not possess the light (truth and holiness) needed for entrance into God's kingdom of heaven. As a result, this verse demands that the good news must be the foundation upon which we, as believers, must build our relationships with all others. This obviously includes you. Believe me, this is not done out of some hidden propagandist agenda. Writing a book of any kind is difficult, but we, as Christians, love you with a divine love and do not want you naively standing in the street as disaster awaits (see Introduction).

You see, to assist or help you in any way without sharing the good news and providing the light you need to enter heaven does not really love you. Why? Love desires the very best for a person and for you is to become a member of the kingdom of God. The very best for you is not allowing you to die in your sins. In Matthew 16:26, the Lord declares, "For what will it profit a man, if he gains the whole world, and forfeits his life [soul]? Or what will a man give in exchange for his life?" Here Jesus indicates that a man will profit nothing if he gains the whole world and loses his true life which extends into eternity.

We, as Christians, cannot just love you into the kingdom of God; we have to present the gospel to you. We can help you, even give advice and money to you, but what will you have gained when you have lost your soul to hell for all eternity? We, as saints, can definitely bless your city and its citizens by cleaning up the trash, rebuilding homes, finding shelter for the homeless, and providing food to the needy, which are all good deeds. Yet, without the gospel presented and accepted, every unbeliever in your city (including you) will perish in their sins into an eternity of darkness without God. Therefore, sharing the good news, by those who look upon the needy world with real compassion, must be the first and most important blessing and aid that we can offer you and the others. A meal to a homeless person lasts about ten minutes, the gospel will last an eternity. The Scriptures call for believers in Jesus Christ to be courageous Christians involved in a lifetime of witness. This book is my witness and the witness of whomever gave this to you of the good news of Jesus Christ. This book has the true message of Jesus found in the Bible (the light of Christ), and it is life-changing.

Though some believe the gospel is not relevant for today's culture, it has been around for over two thousand years doing what it has always done: transforming lives. It is, in and of itself, very relevant. Why? It provides the entrance to heaven thus changing one's eternity and it furnishes the key tool to live life more fully upon this Earth. Though the good news does not promise physical prosperity as man defines it, it is does promise spiritual prosperity as God defines it. It involves what Paul calls all the spiritual blessings in the heavenly places (Ephesians 1:3) and John calls eternal life forever with God (1 John 5:11-12). This begins the moment that someone receives Jesus Christ as Savior and Lord. This book will explain to you exactly how you may receive Him from the Holy Word of God alone not according to some men's imaginations or opinions.

For a period of time, I directed a children's program at my local church that met every Wednesday night. Each club night, parents would come and drop off their children for a fun night of games, Bible teaching, and small group time. Outside of the usual "Hello, How are you?" we would not see the parents at all. It dawned on me that many of these parents probably did not know the Lord. Even if we brought their children to Christ, we would be sending them back into a non-Christian home where Jesus is not honored or taught. Since God's blueprint is to have parents raise their children in the discipline and instruction of the Lord, this could not happen if the parents were unbelievers (Ephesians 6:4).

At the time, there was an evangelistic training program that was sweeping through the churches. Our church had recruited maybe thirty people to be trained in the program and share the gospel. I decided to see if I could weave the two programs together. I contacted the director of the evangelism program and asked him if he could provide me with five teams of two individuals. Each team could visit the homes of my club members and share the gospel with their parents. This called for the creation of a club handbook to explain the program and what their children were doing each night with photos. At the end of the handbook was a gospel message for the club evangelists to use under the heading, "What Your Children Are Learning."

I made each evangelist an official member of the club and gave them a club uniform. Then, they spent several nights assigned to a particular grade level in order to get to know the program and kids. When they felt like they were a real part of the club and had the knowledge to answer not only questions about the good news but about the program, they were sent out into the community of our parents. Each team visited a parent or two a week from their assigned grade level. I would meet with the many teams for bible study and prayer once a month, and they would provide a report on all things God was doing. We discovered that many of the parents went to either our church or a bible church in the area and were true believers. Others were not and with them God did some incredible things. One amazing night, one of our evangelistic teams comprised of a married couple, Ken and Jackie, were invited into a woman's home where it was very obvious that the woman at the door was a single mom and had three toddlers in tow.

They introduced themselves and she did also. Her name was Sara. The couple began their presentation only to be interrupted by these very active toddlers. Ken took the kids into the other room, still in view of mom, and played with them, while Jackie shared the handbook and the gospel with her. Sara said that she had been so busy in her life that she didn't have time to think about herself but wanted her kids to be brought up in church. Jackie explained that care for her children was admirable, but she needed it too.

In that living room, while the kids were laughing and playing in the family room, Sara turned her life over to Jesus Christ as Savior and Lord. Eventually, she started bringing her kids to the nursery we provided and began working with other kids to share the Lord with. Though this is a great story, there were many other parents who rejected the club evangelists or their message. Some were so grateful that we were helping their children but wanted no part of it. Others complained about the "indoctrination," but they were more than willing to send their children anyway.

The evangelists attempted to answer all of their questions gently and with loving attitudes. Each time the parents were asked how we could meet the needs of their children in even a better way. Afterward, as they shared with the larger team and me, we rejoiced and thanked God for the chance to show His love to them.

Why would all these people take their valuable time out of a busy week and share the gospel? It is not because we want to win converts out of some kind of hidden motives. It is because we love and care for people so much that we do not want to see them perish in their sins. We so desire to take the hands of others and lead them out of a disastrous eternity. May we do this for you?

Chapter 2

Acknowledge God's Sovereignty

As I am proclaiming the gospel of Jesus to you right now, you must understand that God is also at work in your heart. This moment is an interaction between you (the human) and God (the divine). As a result, it is important to know from the start that the good news of salvation was all God's idea and will be all God's work in your life as you respond to Him. These beliefs and responses I am about to share are the light that will lead you into heaven. God has compelled me to write this and share it with others. Handing this light over to you through the gospel is also His sovereign work. Then if you choose to follow the light and receive Jesus Christ as Savior and Lord that will also be Him at work in your life.

Paul made this so clear to the Christians in the ancient city of Ephesus. In Ephesians 2:8-9, Paul explains, "For by grace you have been saved through faith, and that not of yourselves; it is the gift of God, not of works, that no one would boast." The Lord will provide you with the power to believe in the necessary truths and the desire to make the necessary responses to be saved. The light to His heaven is faith not works. Yet, works will result from faith.

In the next verse (v. 10) Paul describes it, "For we are his workmanship, created in Christ Jesus for good works, which God prepared before that we would walk in them." Once we are created in Christ, good deeds will flow from it. This will be a growth experience and not happen all at once. It is also a work of the Holy Spirit (Philippians 2:12-13). I tell you this because whatever you have heard about the true gospel or Christianity, it is not meant to be a system of rules or works to earn heaven. You can't work your way into the kingdom of God. The light is based solely on faith that is given by God. Man cannot work his way into heaven no matter how hard he may try. Now, every other religion is based in some way on working your way into heaven. No one can be that good! As you read this book, God may be at work in your life and preparing your heart for this moment.

How? First, through His creation He has been revealing Himself to you ever since you were born (Romans 1:18-20; Psalm 19:1-6). You already know much about the Lord God because you have experienced His goodness, mercy, love, and blessing as you enjoy what He made. Second, He spent several thousand years writing down His message through His prophets and then His Son Jesus in the Bible (Hebrews 1:1-2; John 21:24-25). Third, He has been convicting you of your sin and its judgment through His Spirit and your inner conscience (John 15:26-27). Fourth, God has brought you to this critical moment through a series of circumstances which made you pick up this book (Acts 9:3; Luke 15:14-17).

As He prepared me to write this book, He was preparing you to read it. If someone gave you this book, He prepared them to give it to you. It is all Him. Before Jesus left the Earth, He told them to be His witness (Acts 1:8) throughout the world and make disciples for Him (Matthew 28:19). We are not trying to impose ourselves on you we are following our God. This was His grand idea. Lastly, he created the plan of salvation I am about to explain to you (John 17:4).

If you are to believe, God will open your heart. The Bible describes all people as being spiritually blind (2 Corinthians 4:4), unable to understand spiritual things (1 Corinthians 2:14) and hardened in their hearts toward Him (Ephesians 4:19). In John 6:44, Jesus declares that no one can come to Him unless the Father draws Him. The Lord Jesus brought the Word, and the Father through His Holy Spirit opened their minds. Paul declared the good news of Christ to the Thessalonians. He described it as coming not just in words but in the full conviction of the Spirit and in His power (1 Thessalonians 1:5). Is this happening to you right now?

In Acts 16:14, Paul preached to a woman named Lydia, a seller of purple fabrics, in Philippi. Luke describes it in these words, "A certain woman named Lydia, a seller of purple, of the city of Thyatira, one who worshiped God, heard us; whose heart the Lord opened to listen to the things which were spoken by Paul." Luke discloses that the Lord opened her heart to listen to the things which Paul spoke. He always depended on the Spirit to work in the hearts of his listeners. He knew he could not do this work on his own. Human effort cannot possibly compensate for the supernatural work of the Spirit. I am depending on the Holy Spirit and have prayed for Him to open your heart right now to these Words of His. If you come to Christ, it will be all His work.

Though this is a spiritual work of the Spirit of God, you must hear the message and respond to it appropriately. To enter the kingdom of God in the way He desires, we cannot simply tack Jesus onto a life we already live. Jesus takes over our life. He is not an addition, nor is He a religion, nor is He just a comfortable support in times of crises, or a method to help you flourish in this life. He is a person who must be believed in and obeyed. He is both Savior and Lord. He will place you into His kingdom and you should be ready to live differently and to obey Him in His Word (the Bible).

Sometime ago, I was a pastor of a local church. One day, I was sitting in my office looking out the window enjoying the sunshine as I was studying the Word. Suddenly, I saw two women drive up and get out of their car and knock on the church door. When I opened the door, the younger woman introduced herself as Shirley and her mother's name was Virginia. Tears were flooding from her face and her mother's head was slumped over with her eyes to the ground. She explained that her father, Robert, had just passed away. The daughter looked as if she was in her sixties and the mother was in her eighties. The two of them were both devastated. He passed away from a sudden and unexpected heart attack. Her parents had occasionally attended our church, but it was many years back.

They had nowhere else to go for help with the planning of a religious service. Virginia indicated that they had never really been "church people," but this was the only church she knew. The daughter asked if I could help her mother with the funeral arrangements and then preside over the funeral service. From that moment forward, I began to pray for their salvation as I attended to the arrangements. The daughter did not live in the town or area, so it was just Virginia and I planning the viewing and memorial with the funeral home.

Knowing that God had called me (as every Christian) to share the gospel and offer the light to heaven to everyone, I decided that I would ask her a few questions to determine if either of them had ever received Jesus Christ. They had not. I prayed that God would give me the opportunity to share the gospel with her. I also had to determine the kind of service I would have for Robert. Perhaps, he had become a Christian near the end, and no one knew it.

When the night of viewing her husband's body arrived, I sat next to Virginia and tried to comfort her the best I could. Many people came to pay their respects to her and left in a steady stream. Since Shirley could not make it, it left me alone with her to share the gospel. I felt like it was a divine moment. Deep in my heart I was praying fervently for the opportunity to speak with her that night. I must admit I was fearful as to how I would actually begin the conversation, how I would proceed, and how she would respond. Would the Lord even give me the opportunity that night and would I be courageous enough to take it?

Then the strangest thing happened. After everyone had come and gone, I looked at my watch and there was about ten minutes remaining. I thought, "I better say something quick, or it will be too late!" Suddenly, a tall, large, muscular man walked into the room, looked at her husband's body in the casket, and began frantically pacing the parlor. In a loud, high-pitched, cracking voice, he kept saying, "I don't know what to say. I don't know what to say. I don't know what to say." He walked back and forth from the casket to the door, over and over again, uttering those fateful words, "I don't know what to say." Then, he walked out; he never spoke to us.

I remember thinking, "Wait a minute, I do know what to say. I have a message from the King of Kings and Lord of Lords for this woman." I turned to Virginia and whispered, "Virginia, I would like to leave your wonderful husband into the hands of a holy, loving God for eternity, and I would like to talk about your relationship to God and the life to come. Would that be, okay?" She grabbed my arm, squeezed it, and began to cry. After a few moments, she looked at me and whispered, "Please do. I need to know."

Right there in the viewing room of her deceased husband, while her tears were flowing, I announced the message that God had for her. That night, she received Jesus Christ as Savior and Lord. God in his powerful sovereignty worked everything out so I could share the gospel. I know by faith that her husband had also been given that chance if God so desired. When she did trust the Lord Jesus Christ, I could see the comfort and peace that came over her from the good news.

Before we departed, she said to me, "Please, Pastor, share that message of good news in the memorial service on Saturday because I want everybody to have the hope that Jesus has now given to me." I want to provide this hope for you. Will you accept it?

Chapter 3

Seek Christ's Kingdom

The gospel of Jesus begins with the plan of redemption that I alluded to in the previous chapters. It was ordained in eternity past and fully revealed to man over thousands of years in the Old and New Testaments. It is an amazing story. For you to become a Christian, you must understand and seek Christ's kingdom. This is the first step into the light allowing you to enter the kingdom of heaven. The plan has its roots in the creation of man.

In Genesis chapter two, God described His creation of the Earth, sun, moon, stars, plants, and animals. After this, the Lord God proceeded to fashion and sculpt His greatest creation: man. Here's where we come in. In verse 7, Moses writes that God formed man out of the dust of the ground and then breathed into him the breath of life. As a result, man became a living, thinking being. Out of man, the Lord God formed a woman (Genesis 2:18-25). God placed man and now woman in a beautiful Earthly garden called Eden and walked and talked with the couple in the cool of the day (Genesis 3:8).

Why was Adam and Eve created in the first place (which would eventually lead to us)? Why were they walking and talking with God in the garden in the cool of the day? What was the point? Herein lies the very same questions that people have been struggling with for thousands of years. Why do we exist? What is life all about? Am I going to just happen into the world and happen out of the world and that is it? The answer is found in God's Word. The creation of man was the creation of a kingdom of people by God the Father to honor God the Son. That is right. Our purpose which will bring the joy we seek and the fulfillment we desire is to serve and honor the Son of God.

Let me explain. In John 3:35, John the Baptist describes it this way, "The Father loves the Son, and has given [as a gift] all things into his hand." In John 10:29, the Son, Jesus, portrays His people as sheep and states, "My Father, who has given them [as a gift] to me, is greater than all." In Colossians 1:15-16, the apostle Paul described it in these words, "Who [Jesus] is the image of the invisible God, the firstborn [preeminent one, not first to be born] of all creation. For by him all things were created, in the heavens and on the Earth, things visible and things invisible, whether thrones or dominions or principalities or powers; all things have been created through him, and for him." Notice, the two words "for Him." Everything in the universe was created "for Him." This includes us.

So, as Adam and Eve walked in the garden, they were to be given as a gift to the Son of God by God the Father. In Genesis 1:28, this is the reason they were given a powerful mandate by God when the Lord told them to "Be fruitful, multiply, fill the Earth, and subdue it. Have dominion over the fish of the sea, over the birds of the sky, and over every living thing that moves on the Earth." They were to begin having children, with their children having children until the Earth was filled with human beings. As they and their offspring (us included) did this, they were to be in control of the Earth and develop into many societies in one glorious kingdom of God on Earth who honored the Son.

Who would rule man as man ruled the Earth? The Son of God. Why? It was His kingdom, a gift from the Father. The Son and His kingdom of humans would then live their lives serving and glorifying the Father. All would be done in and through the Holy Spirit. This is a mystery and can't be fully understood. This was to be the triune God (three persons in one essence) at work as they loved each other and us. All of this would be forever as men and women continually ate of the tree of Life in the center of the garden (Genesis 2:9).

In John 17:1-2, as Jesus prays to His Father God before His betrayal, He reveals this gift and plan in His own words, "Jesus said these things, and lifting up his eyes to heaven, he said, 'Father, the time has come. Glorify your Son, that your Son may also glorify you; even as you gave him authority over all flesh, he will give eternal life to all whom you have given him." The Father desires to glorify His Son, and the Son seeks to glorify His Father.

We often hear people describe an all-powerful God who desperately desires honor and glory for Himself. It is much deeper than this. God is not a power-hungry ruler who is desperate for His subjects to honor Him alone; instead, He is a loving God, who desperately wants His Son honored. The Son is a loving God who desperately desires His Father to be honored. The Spirit is a third divine personhood who desires desperately to see the Father and Son glorified. Listen, a careful reading of John chapter seventeen demonstrates that the Father desired to glorify the Son, and He wanted the Son to experience what He had as the Son glorified Him. So, He decided to create a kingdom of people who would glorify His Son as the Son glorified Him. He wanted His only Son to experience the same relationship He had with the Son with a multitude of His "brothers and sisters."

A careful reading and study of Philippians 2:5-8 describes Jesus before His coming to Earth and His relationship with the Father. Let's use an analogy. Within the trinity (three equal persons in only one God) consider the Father as a king and the Son as a Prince. Both Father and Son had all the status and power of kings, yet in position one was above the other.

Both were equal in every way. This king wanted the prince to have subjects who would love Him the way the king loved the prince. There was another prince (Holy Spirit) and he desired both to be honored. All three would equally be honored in the honor of any one of them. Why? They were ultimately one essence. All of this grew out of the great and tremendous love all three had for the other as they interacted with each other in eternity past.

So, what then is our purpose on Earth? It is primarily to live as an important part of a kingdom that glorifies (Psalm 86:9), worships (John 4:23), and serves (Luke 4:8) the Son. We (the Son and His brethren) glorify the Father. This is all done in and through the Holy Spirit which brings all beyond the temporal and mortal to the eternal and immortal. Beyond these purposes people in this kingdom were to fellowship and enjoy interaction with Him, (1 John 1:3; Genesis 3:8) each other and nature (Genesis 1:29-31). They were to be holy, righteous, and blameless before God (Ephesians 1:4), to understand and experience all of God's attributes (Romans 9:22), to reign and rule over Earth in order to honor Him (Genesis 1:28), and to exist forever and ever as His people (Genesis 3:22).

All of this was to occur on Earth which was created for this purpose. The kingdom was an Earthly kingdom without sin, disease, and disharmony. They would live in perfectly created human bodies eating continuously from the Tree of Life forever and ever. This fellowship began in a lush garden with Adam and Eve. Their responsibility was twofold. One they were to subdue the Earth and control it for God's glory. Second, they were to reproduce and populate the entire Earth filled with kingdom people who loved the Son. To aid man in his endeavor, God created myriads and myriads of angels to not only honor the Triune God but to serve man as he accomplished this. This was our original future. If Adam and

Eve followed God, we would be on a perfect Earth with perfect people loving God and one another perfectly. There would be no problems. We would be fully and completely happy and fulfilled every moment of every day into eternity. Unfortunately, (yet, fortunately as we shall see) for mankind it did not work out that way.

At first, things went well for the couple as they walked and talked with God in the Garden of Eden. Then, a disaster occurred. As they went forth to subdue the Earth, they were given one stipulation. They could enjoy all that they had, as long as they did not eat of one tree in the garden. This tree was known as the Tree of Good and Evil (Genesis 2:16-17). God told them that in the day that they disobeyed Him and ate the fruit, they would "die." In the garden was placed the greatest of God's holy angels named Lucifer to assist them. Almost immediately, this angel saw all that God was doing for His Son and desired this for himself. Lucifer wanted the glory, power, and kingdom that were being bestowed on the Son, so he rebelled against God and took a third of the angels with him. Then, he set about to take mankind for himself.

This evil angel turned himself into the form of a serpent, tempted and deceived Eve, and she ate of the fruit of the Tree of Good and Evil. Adam rebelled and ate the fruit also (Genesis 3:1-7). As a result, all mankind fell (1 Corinthians 15:22). No longer could man become the gift of a kingdom for His Son (Colossians 1:13), give God all glory (Romans 8:8), constantly fellowship with Him (Genesis 3:24), be holy, righteous, and blameless before the Holy One (Psalm 51:5; Romans 3:10-18), rule the Earth righteously (Ephesians 2:2), live in harmony with all other people (Genesis 4:7-8; 1 John 3:12) and nature (Genesis 3:7; Romans 8:20-21), and most of all, exist forever in their original human bodies (Ephesians 2:1; Romans 6:23). Mankind had fallen into sin.

Now, man would die as he came under the wrath of God (Romans 1:18; Ephesians 2:3; Hebrews 9:27). People would now experience spiritual death and punishment for all their sins in a hell of fire (Matthew 5:22), a place of unquenchable fire (Matthew 9:23), a furnace of fire (Matthew 13:42), a lake of fire (Revelation 20:10), a place which was created for the Serpent of old and his evil demons (Matthew 25:41). You see, when Satan (formerly Lucifer) rebelled, he took a third of the angels with him. In response, the Lord God created a place for their punishment and judgment which Jesus referred to as (Hell).

Man no longer functioned according to the purposes for which God had created him. The entire human race was now destined for a life of rebellion and an eternity of hell. As a result, instead of God destroying Adam and Eve, the plan of redemption came into effect. Before the very foundation of the world, this plan was worked out in eternity past in the mind of the triune God (Ephesians 1:3-6, 11-12). This plan took into account man's sin. Though man did not have to, nor should he have, nor did God want him to, yet God knew man would sin. He allowed man to rebel and determined that His divine response would be to pour out upon man and woman even greater love, goodness, mercy, grace, and blessing. This would bring greater glory to Him, His Son, and Spirit and blessing to man (Ephesians 1:6).

This would also allow the Lord God to display all of His attributes as He delivered man from his own sinful behavior. In Ephesians 3:10, Paul writes this, "To the intent that now through the assembly [church] the manifold [many aspects of the] wisdom of God might be made known." It is through man's salvation that these numerous facets of His wisdom and nature may be displayed. Then, Paul continues, "To the principalities and the powers in the Heavenly places." The angels and demons (in conjunction with mankind) become the divine audience for God's demonstration of all that He is. This wondrous redemptive plan portrays every aspect of His divine character.

God almighty displayed His love as He sent His Son to die (Romans 5:8), His mercy in turning people away from the punishment of fire (Titus 3:5), His grace as He offered an eternity in heaven (Titus 3:7), His patience as He restrained Himself from the destruction of humanity (1 Timothy 1:16), and His eternal power as He destroyed the evil works of darkness (Hebrews 2:14) and death (1 Corinthians 15:55). Also, God even demonstrated His justice and wrath, which are also two of His attributes. These were displayed as He was compelled within Himself to condemn man to eternal punishment (Romans 9:21-23). This ultimate portrayal of His many qualities brings Him more glory from His creation, which includes the angels and man.

This wonderful plan not only gave God more glory, but it gave people more benefits. It did not simply restore man to his original state but gave to him a better and more excellent existence. Man would be given a brand-new and better Earth to rule (2 Peter 3:10; Revelation 21:1). He would have a closer fellowship with God through the Holy Spirit inside of him (1 Corinthians 3:16; Philippians 2:13). Man and woman would be clothed in the holiness and righteousness of Jesus Christ becoming like Him (1 John 3:2-3).

They would now be able to give God more glory because they had become the objects of His grace (Ephesians 5:18; 1 John 2:27). There would be a much deeper fellowship with each other in Christ (1 John 1:3-4). They could ultimately face death with hope in His Son Jesus who overcame death (John 5:29). A new immortal body would be provided for His own (1 Corinthians 15:20-27). All who know and love Him would inherit all the riches that are in the Son (1 Peter 1:4). These are just a few of the abundant blessings that were given to those in His kingdom. This was fortunate for man.

All this was God's gracious and loving plan in response to man's sinful actions. It had been determined that the Second Person of the Trinity would clothe Himself in humanity and come to Earth to pay the penalty for sin (Philippians 2:5-8; Isaiah 53:6). In Romans 3:23-24, the apostle Paul writes, "For all have sinned, and fall short of the glory of God." Every man and woman commits sin and deserves punishment. Then Paul continues with God's solution, "Being justified freely by his grace through the redemption that is in Christ Jesus."

Though the plan had been originated in eternity past, God had decided that he would wait to reveal the plan at the moment and in the way He desired. This is His kingdom, and He decides when and how we are to enter it. When man fell God cursed the Earth, threw him out of the garden, and promised that a seed (descendent) of Eve would crush the serpent and finally have victory. This was the first mention of God's plan of redemption. Once man was thrown out of the garden direct communication with God became limited to a few leaders and prophets and people would eventually age and die.

Man became so evil that God had finally had enough and flooded the Earth saving only eight people. To keep Himself from doing this over and over again, God made a covenant evidenced by a rainbow with Noah and the human race began again. Though God told man to multiply and fill the Earth, a descendent of Noah named Nimrod refused. He wanted to create a city, a nation, and a new religion, which had nothing to do with God. As he and many of the other descendants of Noah stood firm building a capitol city and a tower to make sacrifices to this false god (Satan), the Lord scattered them over the Earth diversifying their languages so they could not accomplish this arrogant and evil act. Over the years God eventually abandoned man as he continually rebelled against Him (Romans 1:18-32). As a result of man's sin, the trouble of God's curses, the flood, the dispersion, and then His ultimate abandonment came upon the Earth. Basically, all evil broke loose upon the Earth.

If people so desired to rebel against Him, then they would have to suffer the consequences of that very rebellion. For several thousand years, the Almighty called out a people unto Himself who would be His nation to share His plan of redemption to the world. This nation was Israel. During the days of the Old Testament (the first large section of the Bible), God spoke to His people about His coming Savior. There would be signs and wonders that would identify Him because the Son of God would appear as a man. Over those years, God desired not only Israel but the nations around them to see His work in Israel's life and come to believe in Him. The Lord God continually spoke through His prophets such Moses, David, Solomon, Isaiah, Jeremiah, and others.

Unfortunately, Israel was not faithful to God. After many warnings through the prophets, they were punished. First their nation was divided into two and then each of them was destroyed by conquering nations. When the Medes and Persians took over the majority of the then known world, King Cyrus allowed several leaders (Ezra and Nehemiah) to return to their land and rebuild. After much struggle, Israel was a nation again. Then the Lord God became silent for four hundred years.

After this time, the last of God's Old Testament prophets arose, John the Baptist. He proclaimed to the people of Israel that the promised Messiah (anointed one in the Hebrew) had arrived. He declared that people should repent of their evil deeds and prepare their hearts for the kingdom of God to be restored on the Earth. Jesus (the) Christ (anointed one in the Greek) arrived on the scene in Israel in the first century and claimed to be the Son of God in human form. He was both God and man. His mother conceived Him by the Holy Spirit for this to occur.

For approximately three years Jesus declared that He was the Son of God and only Savior of the world. He offered Israel and all others the opportunity to become a member of God's kingdom by believing in Him. He performed many miracles and fulfilled many prophecies mentioned in the Old Testament concerning His birth, life, and even death. He Himself also predicted His suffering, death, and resurrection from the dead. He gathered together twelve men who would become his spokesmen (the twelve apostles) while He was alive and one (Paul, an apostle of a different kind) after He rose from the dead (Matthew 10:1-4; Galatians 1:1).

The leaders and people hated Him for His righteousness. They despised Him because Jesus made Himself out to be God. They had developed a perfect little man-made works system to get themselves into heaven and refused to believe in this carpenter's son no matter what He said and did. So, they sought to put the Lord Jesus to death. After escaping their clutches on many occasions, the time had come. Judas, one of the twelve, disclosed the place where Jesus would have been located late in the night. So, the Jewish leaders dragged Him before various officials to condemn Him.

When they could not find any law, he had broken, they asked Him outright if He was the Son of God and Jesus declared that He was. This was enough. This man Jesus from Nazareth was blaspheming their God. Since only the Romans could kill Him, the Jews brought Him before the Roman Governor Pilate. Though Pilate tried to dissuade them, they would not stop calling for his death. Finally, he condemned

Jesus Christ to death on a cross (the most humiliating and excruciating death one could have). Once dead, two of His secret disciples asked permission to take the body and bury it properly. This they did in one of their own tombs. The Jews feared that the disciples would steal the body and then claim Jesus resurrected from the dead and begged Pilate to seal the tomb and post a unit of guards in front of it.

The stone covering the tomb would have been about two tons and would have been rolled into place by a gulley they would have dug. Yet, though He died on a Friday evening, by Sunday, He had risen! This would be counted as three days by the Jews just as Christ had predicted. Jesus began to appear to His disciples and to others for many days to make sure the world knew that He had risen from the dead. Paul tells us He had even appeared to over five hundred people at one time (1 Corinthians 15:6).

The Jewish leaders were so dismayed that they paid the guards who had been knocked out by an angel to keep their mouths shut. They circulated the deceptive story that the body of Jesus had been stolen by His disciples. After forty days of providing His apostles many proofs, He ascended into heaven and told them to proclaim His message and resurrection. In both verbal and written form, they declared that Jesus lived a perfect life and became the perfect sacrifice to pay for our sins. In Christ's death, God punished His only Son instead of man. If men believed in Jesus as the one and only Savior of the world and submitted their lives to Him as Lord, they could enter the kingdom of God forever. If man did not receive Him, then they would have to spend an eternity without God, His Father.

This is the plan of redemption. They proclaimed it to that generation and then wrote it down in the New Testament so every generation could hear the good news of Jesus Christ.

Now, I am proclaiming it to you. You see, when Jesus came, He proclaimed this plan of redemption which involved His physical death on the cross and His resurrection. After this, He recruited others to proclaim this good news for all people (Matthew 28:19-20; Acts 1:1-8). All believers must be sharing the gospel message. If someone gave you this book, it was because they cared about you, and it pleases the Lord.

Now that you have heard about the kingdom, your first response is to believe in and then seek it. You must desire to be a part of the kingdom of His Son. Essentially, this entails the acceptance of His offer. When the Lord was explaining to the people that in His kingdom they did not need to be concerned about clothing and food, He asserted that they should be seeking the kingdom of God. In Matthew 6:33, He declared with authority, "But seek first God's Kingdom, and his righteousness; and all these things will be given to you as well."

This is the first step in finding the light. This is why Jesus, the Lord, told them that if they seek His kingdom, they would find it (Matthew 7:7; Luke 11:9-10). In Luke 15:8, Jesus Christ characterized true believers as those who sought His kingdom like one searching for a lost coin. She lit a lamp, cleaned the house, and diligently sought to find the coin. The Greek word that is translated "seek" means "to crave, demand, and strive after." These people will deeply desire to be in the kingdom and to live it out. This is why they repent of their sins and begin to seek His righteousness. They want to behave like children of the kingdom. Will you take the first step which is seeking His kingdom? If yes, then let us move on. If not, save this book for later.

Over the years, I have taught weekly Bible studies on a variety of topics. On one such evening, we studied the story of Jesus and the two thieves crucified with Him. Each thief responded differently to the Lord Jesus while He was on the cross. One thief continued to taunt Jesus telling Him to save Himself if He was indeed the Son of God, while the other chastised the first and proclaimed their guilt for the crimes. He begged Jesus to remember him when He entered His kingdom. Jesus responded by telling him that very day he would be with the Lord in paradise. After the description of the mercy and grace shown the repentant thief that night as he now anticipated paradise forever with his new Savior and Lord, everyone was deeply moved. After the evening was over, April, one of the women who attended, began to tell me the story of her grandmother. She was visiting from a small mountain community across the state and had recently lost her husband. She had flown down to see her family and friends in our area, and April had felt a deep burden for her salvation.

The woman tried to share the gospel with her but could not seem to articulate it clearly enough. She realized that she needed some serious training in evangelism and by the time she received it, it would be too late. Her grandmother was older, and it was becoming more and more difficult to make the trip down. April had several small children at home, and it would be extremely difficult to leave them to make the trip to the mountains for even a short time. Then she begged me to speak with her grandmother about the Lord Jesus. I told her that I would share the gospel with her if April would watch and learn how to share the good news for herself. I wanted her to have the privilege of bringing people to Christ also. I wanted her to feel the thrill of being used by God.

We decided that April would invite me over for coffee on the following Saturday and her husband would take the kids to the park while we visited with her grandmother. When I arrived, April introduced me to her grandmother, Donna. After a few minutes of casual conversation, I inquired about her religious background and her understanding of Christ. Since I could not find a specific way within the conversation to introduce the good news, I went to my back up plan. I just simply asked, "In our Bible study we discussed last week the story of the thief on the cross, and it was amazing. Would you like to study that story with us for a few minutes?"

When the Holy Spirit has prepared a heart for salvation, it is like a piece of fruit falling effortlessly into your hand. It doesn't have to be yanked and pulled. We began by reading the story with each of us taking a turn. Periodically, I would stop the reading and explain the verse bringing in every point of the gospel. Since Donna was listening so intensely, I could tell the Spirit was at work and preparing her to receive Christ. When we finished, I asked her if she would desire to receive Christ as Savior and Lord. Donna looked at me and smiled saying, "I have been waiting for Him my whole life. Yes, I would." We prayed the prayer of salvation as April, her granddaughter, prayed silently and rejoiced. I wrote in the Bible which I had given her the date of her salvation.

We talked together about her new life in Christ and the importance of finding a group of true believers in her area to support her. When I left, I was once again amazed at what God could do in a person's heart. She went back to her little mountain town and got involved with a local Bible believing church and made many friends and served the Lord. Several years after, I performed her memorial service describing that day she came to our Lord. We rejoiced knowing that she was in heaven. The granddaughter told me that now she couldn't wait to start sharing the gospel herself. This granddaughter had sought the kingdom of heaven and found it. Will you?

Chapter 4

Turn From Your Sin

Today, many people believe they are basically good and will be in a better place when they die. Others believe that they do not have to worry about death because somehow it will all work out to a happy conclusion. Still others simply do not concern themselves about death because they feel nothing can be done to prevent it. Some have decided that they will not worry since no one knows what will happen anyway.

These denials cannot change the reality of their judgment and condemnation for a lifetime of sin. Those who have not received Christ, thus appropriating His death on the cross for their wicked deeds, will not be saved from this judgment. This is a harsh and terrifying reality that I must declare to you. Yes, it is offensive, but much more offensive would be you finding yourself in an eternity of hell and punishment. So, the second step to entering heaven is to "turn from sin."

In Romans 3:10-11, Paul explains that there is no one who is righteous or understands God. In Romans 3:23, he asserts that all have sinned and fall short of God's glory. This sin brought God's condemnation. Then in chapter 6:23, Paul writes, "For the wages of sin is death." This is both physical and eternal. This truth is preached by Jesus and His apostles in every one of their gospel messages; therefore, to follow their example, I must proclaim it to you.

This declaration began with John the Baptist preparing the Jews for Christ's arrival. In Mark 1:4, Mark writes, "John came baptizing in the wilderness and preaching the baptism of repentance for forgiveness of sins." This last prophet of the

Old Testament preached repentance. The repentance was from the sin that brought judgment.

In Luke 3:7-21, Luke describes more fully John's message. In answer to their questions of what they must do to show their repentance, John the Baptist indicted them for being selfish toward others less fortunate. The tax collectors were accused of gauging people by overcharging them. Soldiers were blamed for their lies and false charges, extorting others by threatening them with violence, and not being content with their wages. He even indicted Herod the Tetrarch for having an illicit relationship with his brother's wife, which got him thrown in jail and ultimately beheaded. In Matthew 3:7-9, the apostle Matthew records that the Baptist called the Pharisees and Sadducees the offspring of snakes and vipers who depended on being descendants of Abraham to save them from their constant wickedness.

Though people think Jesus preached only love, this is not the case. He indicted people for their wickedness. When the Lord Jesus was seating at a well waiting for the disciples to purchase food for their journey, He encountered a woman who came to draw water. He told her that He had living water that she could drink that would spring up to eternal life. When she requested that living water (the gospel), He began to confront her wicked living. In John 4:16-18, Christ responded with a scathing description of her sin, "Jesus said to her, 'Go, call your husband, and come here.' The woman answered, 'I have no husband.' Jesus said to her, 'You said well, 'I have no husband,' for you have had five husbands; and he whom you now have is not your husband. This you have said truly.'" He did not yell or berate her; He gently confronted her to order to give her the perfect opportunity to repent of her many sins. The indictment of sin was never to crush people but to offer them repentance and salvation.

In John 8, evil men came and cast an adulterous woman before the Lord Jesus. Then, they asked Him if she should be stoned to death. Jesus responded by writing their sins on the ground with a stick and asked those who were sinless to cast the first stone. These accusers needed to deal with their own sin before they dealt with hers. They refused and left leaving the woman there alone. In John 8:11, the Lord commanded the adulterous woman to "Go your way. From now on, sin no more." (John 8:11). He did not try and conceal her sins or theirs. This entire scene involved the exposure of the sins of people and the opportunity to find salvation through Jesus, not condemnation. Judgment comes when people will not recognize their sin and embrace Jesus as Savior and Lord in order for their sins to be forgiven.

In Matthew 23:13-36, the Lord Jesus called the Pharisees and scribes "hypocrites, pretenders, blind fools and guides, cups who are only clean on the outside and dirty on the inside, white tombs full of dead men's bones." Of course, His harsher language was always reserved for hypocritical false enslaving teachers, but Jesus always indicted people for sin. Once the indictment came, the gospel writers mention his proclamation for people to repent (Matthew 4:17; 12:41; Luke 5:32; Luke 13:3-5). In their repentance came the forgiveness they needed to enter heaven.

Every evangelist who preached in the book of Acts spoke of this condemnation. They never left it out. In Acts 14:15, Paul arrives in Lystra, heals a man, and he and Barnabas are hailed as gods. Paul is given a chance to speak and entreats them to turn away from their useless and vain idol worship. In Acts 26:18, Paul is preaching the gospel to King Agrippa and explains that belief in Christ will bring him forgiveness of sins and an inheritance in heaven. Again, we see Paul offering God's kingdom after he indicts them for their sins. How can they repent without knowing they were sinners?

You see, Christians must speak of this coming judgment. This does not mean we do not sin also and deserve the same judgment. We do, but we have been forgiven of all our sins. The apostle Paul declares that believers have passed out of condemnation in eternal life (Romans 8:1). You can do the same. Yet as a loving Father, God does discipline us for the evil we do and trains us to live righteously (Hebrews 12:4-8). So, we are not attempting to be hypocrites when we speak of the sins of others to bring them to a point of repentance. We are well aware that we too are sinners, we simply do not want to see them, or you die in sin and be separated from God for all eternity.

In Acts 17:30-31, Paul travels to Athens and he preaches that the Athenians must repent of their sin for condemnation was coming. Paul, the apostle, proclaimed the gospel and continually indicted people for their wickedness and then proclaimed a coming judgment. To find the light and enter heaven you must deal with your own personal sins.

As Christians, we cannot replace judgment from sin by proclaiming to you that Jesus can fulfill one or more of your felt needs. To seriously ask you to place your faith in Jesus Christ because the Lord will satisfy your needs is preaching contrary to the message of Jesus and the apostles. God does not always fulfill every felt need. Often, Christianity brings persecution and trials. Our lives may actually become more complicated since we are now moving against the flow of life. Yet, God Almighty will fulfill your deepest longings for Him which He put in your heart.

So, what is this judgment of sin to come? Though hinted at in the Old Testament, Jesus Christ clearly explained a future punishment to come. The Lord Jesus did speak of God's love, grace, and mercy, but Christ also spoke of the coming judgment for wickedness and declared that all must repent of their wickedness and believe in Him (Matthew 4:17; Mark 1:15). He portrayed a future judgment of sin in frighteningly vivid descriptions. The judgment of sin would be everlasting punishment in a place He called "Hell." The word translated "Hell" comes from the Greek term "Gehenna." Gehenna was a place outside Jerusalem where the Hebrew people threw all their garbage. It was the trash heap and garbage dump of Israel. This was a disgusting place where the people's refuse would be burned continually producing a horrid and putrid smell (Matthew 5:22).

Jesus painted a picture of condemnation for sin as human beings smoldering in a supernatural, putrid garbage dump for all eternity. That is not all. He uses other descriptions equally horrifying. He proclaimed that hell was a place of "unquenchable fire" (Matthew 3:12; Mark 9:43; Luke 3:17). It was a location of a burning fire (Matthew 13:40) and a fiery furnace (Matthew 13:50). It was a dwelling with an eternal inferno (Matthew 18:8) where weeping (from the sorrow and pain endured continually) and gnashing of teeth (from the agony and anguish of suffering with torment forever) exist continually without relief (Matthew 8:12; 13:42, 50; 22:13; 24:51; 25:30; Luke 13:28).

Hell was an abode designed for the "destruction of body and soul" (Matthew 10:28) in a vicinity of complete "outer darkness" (Matthew 22:13). The apostles added their own terrifying descriptions. In 2 Thessalonians 1:9, Paul adds the image of a region where its occupants are "continually and everlastingly destroyed." In Revelation 14:10-11, John depicts hell as a place where its inhabitants will be "tormented with fire and brimstone" and the "smoke of their torment would go up forever and ever" with "no rest day or night."

Then in Revelation 20:14, the apostle John describes this state of punishment as the "second death." The first one is physical dying and temporal separation from all we know and love. This second death will be eternal separation from everyone we know. We will be completely alone.

Why must man face this punishment? The key is found in Revelation 4:10. Here John discloses that those in hell "will drink of the wine of the wrath of God." This wine will be "prepared unmixed in the cup of His anger." The almighty God of the universe will be angry and those who sin will experience His wrath for all eternity. Why is God so angry? Again, people hear about the love, grace, and mercy of God, but rarely do they hear about His holiness, righteousness, and justice.

These key attributes are just as much a part of His divine nature as His love, grace, and mercy. This has made people think that God is only wonderful and sweet and never wrathful. Yet, this is not so! As mankind views himself as a composite of many attributes, so God must be seen in the same way. God is angry because He Himself and His laws are so righteous and holy, but man is utterly unrighteous and unwilling to follow His laws. Let me explain.

The Old Testament speaks often of the absolute holiness, righteousness, and justice of God (Psalm 89:14,18). When His Son Jesus came, He also revealed these attributes about His Father which He Himself possessed (John 17:11; 17:25; John 5:30). Jesus also demonstrated these divine characteristics in such actions as the cleansing of the temple (God's holiness - John 2:14-17), the harsh condemnation of the Jewish leaders (God's righteousness - Matthew 23:13-36), and the preaching of the coming judgment of all men (God's justice - Matthew 12:36; John 5:22, 27, 30; 12:31). He announced to the world that some would rise from the grave to a resurrection of life and the rest would rise to a resurrection of judgment (John 5:29).

Let us look at each of these divine attributes separately for a moment. The Lord God of the universe is holy. This Greek word translated holy means "wholly separate from." God is wholly different and separate from man. He is "righteous" and does only "good." As we have seen, man and woman had the opportunity to be holy and good from their creation onward (Genesis 2:15-17). But they disobeyed the command of God and they (including me and you) have been rebelling against Him ever since (Genesis 3:6). This disobedience of His law is called "sin." The Greek word translated sin means "to miss the mark." Any disobedience of His law misses God's mark whether humans like it or not. The Lord sets the standard, not man. According to James, any disobedience of the law breaks not just one but the whole law (James 2:10).

This disobedience to God and the breaking of even one of His laws is utterly and completely wicked and unrighteous. It deserves a horrible and terrible punishment. Why? God is utterly righteous and completely just. His righteousness and justice must demand a penalty (Romans 1:18; 2:5). When this occurred, His love, grace, and mercy surfaced, and a divine provision was made. Someone else would take man's place. Someone who never transgressed Him, who never deserved punishment, and fulfilled the entire law of God, would be substituted in rebellious man's place to receive this awful punishment from God. This person would be born, live, and experience God's full wrath to satisfy His justice for sin (John 1:29; 3:16; Hebrews 9:22). This substitute would have to be divine for it to be eternal and supernatural. He would have to be human for it to be a true replacement. As a result, Jesus took on human flesh to die for us (John 1:1, 14).

As the God-Man, He paid the penalty for our sins in His death on the cross. God made only one provision for people to appropriate what His Son did on the cross for them. This provision is the repentance of sin and faith in Jesus Christ as only Savior of the world and Lord of their lives. People must stand humbly before this holy, righteous, and just God. They must acknowledge that He is full of anger and wrath for their constant sin and disobedience. They must repent of all their wickedness and receive Jesus Christ as Savior and Lord. They must believe He is God's Son and only Savior of the world. They must ask Him to save them and submit their lives to Him as Lord and Master.

When they do this, all their sins, past, present, and future will be forgiven and washed away in God's love, grace, and mercy. In His love, grace, and mercy, He pursues everyone. The Lord continually reveals Himself through creation and conscience. Then He presents His message of good news concerning salvation in His Son to all who respond through those who already know Him (Christians). Yet, His holiness, righteousness, and justice will not allow the substitution to take place unless there is repentance and belief. This means that those who refuse to repent and acknowledge Jesus as His Son, Savior, and Lord will perish into hell forever.

Once saved from this eternal hell, He requires submission to His Son as Lord and obedience to His commandments as demonstrations of true faith all throughout His children's mortal lives. In His love, grace, and mercy, He continually forgives their transgressions. In His holiness, righteousness, and justice, He disciplines and trains His children to be like Him in every way.

His goal is for all His children to grow up spiritually to think, speak, and act exactly like Jesus, His beloved Son. This would be to think, speak, and act just like Him. All of this can be fully accomplished through the power of His Spirit who lives within them. This thinking, speaking, and acting just like Him not only occurs in their personal lives but in their interactions with each other and those outside the faith.

Though this cannot be fully accomplished in this life, it is the striving after it that God desires.

You must understand that Revelation (the last book in the Bible about the end of the world and beyond) ends with the judgment of those who have never had their sins forgiven. This judgment can only be avoided through a gospel that proclaims it. In Revelation 20:12, the apostle John describes it, "I saw the dead, the great and the small, standing before the throne, and they opened books. Another book was opened, which is the book of life. The dead were judged out of the things which were written in the books, according to their works." There will be a wrath filled with condemnation for every single sin ever committed by those who have not responded to the Lord Jesus appropriately. It is a frightening prospect that cannot be avoided. So, we who share the good news (as I am with you right now) are compelled to give the bad news first. Otherwise, it is not really good news.

In our bad news, I must address your sin and judgment for you to see your desperate need for salvation. The bottom line is that you are a sinner and must acknowledge your sins to God. You have broken God's laws. You might ask, "What laws?" You know what you have done as I know what I have. Your heart has been constantly convicting you and you must listen. This is called the "conscience" that God has put inside of us so we will know our own sins and repent (Romans 2:15). Also, if the Lord God Almighty is calling you into Christ's kingdom, the Holy Spirit is convicting you right now (John 16:8).

The key is to recognize that you are wicked and a sinner; then you should repent. True repentance will result from a real understanding of the absolute holiness of God, His Son, and Spirit. No person can be saved without full repentance, which demonstrates true belief. In 2 Timothy 2:24-26, Paul exhorts Timothy, his son in the faith, to gently correct those who are opposing him. Why? Perhaps, God will cause them to repent and lead them into the knowledge of the truth. In Matthew 3:2, John the Baptist declared people should repent because the kingdom of God was at hand.

In Matthew 4:17, the apostle reveals that the ministry of the Lord Jesus was also the preaching of repentance and the proclaiming of the kingdom of God. One's repentance is a key to entering the kingdom of God. It is an essential part of the salvation response. There are three critical aspects to this concept of "repentance" in the Scripture. This holy truth involves admitting that you have sinned, sorrowing over your evil doing, and turning away from those sins toward righteousness.

The first is the admission of sin. People must admit that they have sinned. John discloses this important aspect as he deals with some in the church that had decided they had matured past sin. He begins in 1 John 1:8 and 10 by saying these people are liars and deceivers of themselves. In verse 9, he provides a characteristic of Christians. The saints confess their sins and find forgiveness. The Greek word translated "confess" literally means to say the same thing. Confession is "to say the same thing about sin" that God says. We are to acknowledge the sins we know we have committed before God and admit they are against His righteous law.

When Jesus encountered a rich young ruler, he claimed to have kept all the law from his youth up. Could that be true? No, he simply refused to admit his sin. Paul described this wretched condition in Romans 1:18; he was suppressing the truth in unrighteousness. Perhaps, so much so that he had convinced himself he was able to keep the whole law. So, Jesus told him to sell all he had which he refused to do. This manifested the real sin in his heart (greed), which was not displayed in any way outwardly (Mark 10:17-31; Matthew 19:16-30; Luke 18:18-30). He had to come to Christ admitting that he was a sinner, which he refused to do. Instead, this rich young ruler left Jesus with his self-righteousness intact but not saved.

The second is to mourn over sins. In the Beatitudes, Jesus says that a characteristic of those in the kingdom of God is mourning. This word speaks of mourning over the dead. In that passage, it has a spiritual application. The word implies mourning over sins and their consequence of spiritual death. When someone receives the Lord, they admit their sin and mourn, grieve, and sorrow over it.

In 1 Corinthians, Paul describes the sins and difficulties this church encountered because they had been prideful and rebellious. Paul was terribly hurt because the church had taken a stand against him. False prophets had risen up and found a leader in the church. This leader with most of the church stood against Paul and his ministry. So, he sent the difficult and confrontational letter of 1 Corinthians. When he visited, they did not respond well so he shortened his visit and departed. Later, Paul sent Titus to discover their final response to him and his many words of rebuke. When Titus returned, he brought good news of the church's repentance for standing against Paul.

In 2 Corinthians 7:9-10, Paul describes how much sorrow the church had over their sin. He says, "I now rejoice, not that you were made sorry, but that you were made sorry to repentance. For you were made sorry in a godly way that you might suffer loss by us in nothing. For godly sorrow works repentance to salvation which brings no regret. But the sorrow of the world works death." This sorrow was a godly sorrow which produced a real repentance leading to salvation. This is the sorrow that Christians have when they come to Christ. This is the sorrow Christians have when they live for Christ. The first leads to initial salvation and the other to final eternal salvation. This is the true sorrow over sin that eternally saves. This is the sorrow that produces real repentance.

This is the sorrow that was expressed by the woman who came to Jesus in Luke 7:37-39. This grieving woman washed His feet with her tears and wiped them with her hair. What sorrow over sin! The repentant woman kissed His feet and anointed them with expensive perfume. What humility and mourning over wrong-doing!

Also in the Corinthian passage, Paul describes a sorrow that only leads to death. This sorrow is one that produces bitterness, despair, anger, and pride. This sorrow lashes out at the other person for hurting them, rebuking them, or interrupting their sin. It vents at oneself in punishment and self-hatred. It will not plead for forgiveness.

Third is the repentance of sins. Though this word is used with a fuller meaning in defining the entire concept, it also has a unique meaning of its own. The Greek word translated repent means to turn around in the other direction or change one's mind or behavior. One must turn around from sin and go in the opposite direction.

Luke records Peter's denial of knowing the Lord Jesus in Luke 22:62 and how the apostle wept in great sorrow and remorse afterward. Later, Luke records in Acts chapter two, three, and other passages the numerous sermons that Peter preached in great boldness for the Lord Jesus Christ. Peter demonstrated that he had turned in the opposite direction from that grievous sin. Of course, the Spirit of God provides the strength and power needed to accomplish this spiritual and supernatural feat (Acts 2:4; Romans 8:13).

Contrast that with Judas. In Matthew 27:3-9, he would not repent before the Lord Jesus, nor would he humble himself before Jesus. Judas refused to request any forgiveness, thus removing the guilt and sorrow. Instead, he killed himself to alleviate them from his life. This is the sorrow unto death. At times, the saints might not want to offend their unsaved acquaintances, neighbors, and friends so they will leave out this important saving step in their presentations. Instead, they will replace it with the hurt or sorrow these unbelievers may feel over their unmet needs, trials, or difficulties. They offer Jesus as the great healer, who will save them from their unfulfilled lives.

This is not the gospel. This will not allow those hearing the message to view Jesus Christ as the righteous judge and Holy One. The Lord will save them from their punishment for unrighteousness and bring them safely to an eternal, supernatural life, not a comfortable, temporal life. So, if you desire to enter heaven, you must admit before God that you are a sinner (even naming the major ones), sorrow over those sins, and commit yourself to acting differently. This "acting differently" will come increasingly as you grow more like Him and spiritually mature in your Christian life. It does not happen overnight.

One of the joys of my life has been teaching at junior high summer church camps. I would share from God's Word each morning and evening. From the day I left the last camp to the day I entered the next camp a year later, I prayed for unsaved souls to see their sins, repent, and come to Christ and saved ones to recommit their lives to obedience to Him or to rededicate themselves fully to greater spiritual growth. I wanted this time to be a life changing experience through the power of the Word, prayer, and the Holy Spirit. My team would always arrive the day before to plan, prepare, and pray. I will never forget the year our caravan of cars entered the camp's parking lot and just beyond it we saw a sea of green moving through the camp.

The camp director waved his arms to stop us. When I rolled down the window to ask him what was going on, he looked at me blankly and said ominously, "Frogs! Hundreds and hundreds of frogs have just stormed into the camp!" I could not believe my ears. I jokingly said, "Did you change my camp theme to the Exodus out of Egypt?" He stared at me and told me that he was not joking. The camp had been virtually taken over by little green frogs about three inches long.

He explained that as soon as the last bus of kids from the previous week's camp drove off the lot, the frogs began to appear. He was completely baffled by it all and wondered what I wanted to do about it. I had spent a year praying for these students, I was not about to leave. I asked him if had called animal control and asked if they were dangerous in anyway. They had told him that at worst they would simply be an annoyance and get into everything.

Then I told him to step aside, it was obvious to me that something spiritual was happening in the heavenly places. I remember thinking, "Where did those words come from?" I was raised in the suburbs. I do not like creatures of any kind, but this was something different. I knew then and there that the forces of darkness were attempting to stop this camp and keep the very students I had been praying for during the last 365 days from coming to Jesus Christ. As the staff got out of our caravan of cars, it was like stepping into a science fiction movie. Frogs were everywhere.

I immediately called for a time of prayer even before we unpacked right there in the parking lot as these frogs were jumping all around. The ten of us who had arrived early prayed for God's strength and power. We cried to the Lord for those whom Satan was trying to stop from coming to Christ, rededicating their lives, or moving to the next level in their spiritual growth. Though we did not know them by name, our blessed Lord did. We asked Him to remove the frogs or help us deal with them wisely. We prayed that the students would not be bothered by them if He allowed them to stay. Then we requested that the Lord would strengthen, our resolve to reach these young people for Christ.

I told the director that nothing in the program was going to change; we would simply trust the Lord and pray. We would pray with all our hearts. When the teens arrived, they thought it was kind of cool to have frogs around. They played with them the first and second day, but by the third, the frogs were virtually ignored. In the midst of this reptile commotion, I kept teaching His Word, speaking of their need for repentance from sin, and sharing the gospel. Often times, we may think that young people will not respond to an approach that deals with indicting them for sin, but it is the gospel. On the third night, the Holy Spirit began to work.

I have never quite seen such powerful conviction by the Holy Spirit. After the evening teaching, the students had an hour of free time before curfew. The camp suddenly became quiet. Everywhere the young people were in small groups praying, crying, repenting, and talking about their lives and Jesus Christ. They were taking the good news that I had presented and were sharing it with their friends. The others around them were praying. In other groups, some were confessing their lack of commitment to their Lord Jesus and how they were going to really live for Him.

It looked like a scene out of a disaster movie. These teens had been convicted and the Holy Spirit was at work in a supernatural way saving lives. By the following Saturday, many young people had come to Christ and others had rededicated themselves to living for Him. When the last bus rolled out, I began praying for next year's group. In the weeks and months following, I received many letters which described how thankful they were to have met someone willing to talk about their sin and how free from its burden they felt. Nothing can stop the Lord's work, not even a camp full of frogs! Will you repent of your sin?

Chapter 5

Believe in Christ's Deity

Jesus Christ is the Son of God! Jesus is God! The third step to enter the kingdom of heaven is to "believe" in Jesus Christ's deity. What does this mean? There are three persons in one Godhead or three personalities in one deity (Matthew 3:16-17; Ephesians 2:18; 1 Peter 1:2). We call this the Trinity (Tri-unity): Father, Son, and Holy Spirit. This is a mystery which cannot be understood by our finite minds. Though the word "Trinity" is not in the Bible, the truth is clearly stated. The true gospel message concerns itself with proclaiming Jesus Christ as God. This is what I am declaring to you right now. In John 8:58, Jesus told the Jews that before Abraham was born, He existed (I Am). This is a direct claim to be the God or Yahweh (I Am) of the Old Testament. The Jews knew this. Next, they took up stones to kill him for blasphemy.

In Mark 14:61, Jesus stood before the Sanhedrin. When asked if He was the Christ, the Son of the Blessed One, He replied with the "I Am." This was the designation of Yahweh of the Old Testament. The high priest's response was the tearing of his robes to signify blasphemy. Declaring oneself as the Son of God was a pronouncement of deity. In John 10:30, when Jesus declared that He and the Father were one (essence), He was proclaiming His deity.

The apostles proclaimed His deity. In Acts 2:36, Peter said, "Let all the house of Israel therefore know certainly that God has made him both Lord and Christ, this Jesus whom you crucified." The apostle Peter, as he was speaking before the multitude at Pentecost, declared that Jesus was both Lord and Christ. In Acts 3:14-15, Peter healed the lame man; then he proclaimed Jesus as the Holy, Righteous One, and the Prince of Life. These were all designations of His deity. In Acts 4:12, Peter boldly announced to the Sanhedrin that only in the name of Jesus could one be saved! This can only be done by deity. In Acts 8, the eunuch from Ethiopia was reading a messianic passage from Isaiah. Philip revealed that it referred to Jesus as the Messiah. This was the proclamation of His deity. From chapter 9 through the entire book, Paul receives Christ and preaches His deity. The book of Acts has many examples.

Now, Christ's humanity is assumed but critical. He was a man of human history. No one questions this. Yet, you must belief he was fully human and fully God. Jesus was the God-Man. Belief in His full humanity as an essential salvation belief was declared when aberrations of this truth arose (1 John 4:2; 2 John 1:7; Heb. 5:7). It was fully assumed before the need to declare it arose.

To be saved, your response to my proclamation of Christ as God must be belief in Christ's deity. No one can be saved unless that person believes Jesus Christ is God, one with the Father as His Only Son (John 8:58-59; 10:30). In 1 John 2, the author John is speaking about some "so-called believers" who call themselves Christians but don't believe in the deity of Jesus, only in His humanity. In verse 22, John calls them liars. If they do not confess the Son, they do not confess the Father.

In 1 John 3:23, John explains to his readers that God's key commandment is to believe in the name of His Son, Jesus Christ. He writes, "This is his commandment, that we should believe in the name of his Son, Jesus Christ, and love one another, even as he commanded." Then, in chapter 5, verses 9-13, John explains that the Lord has testified concerning His Son, Jesus Christ. If one does not believe in the Son, he calls God a liar and does not have eternal life. This doctrine of the deity of Christ must be fully believed. This full belief issues forth in all the other aspects.

The classic passage which verifies this important truth is John 3:16. Here Jesus declared, "For God so loved the world, that he gave his one and only Son, that whoever believes in him should not perish, but have eternal life." Someone must "believe." John finishes his proclamation of the good news in his book by declaring Jesus had performed many other signs that were not written in the gospel, but the ones that were written were to prove Jesus is the Christ, the Son of God (John 20:30-31). God did not expect anyone to simply believe blindly but gave powerful evidence which His Holy Spirit uses to convince and confirm this in our hearts. We will see these later. Eternal life comes from believing that Christ is the Son.

This is the "belief" Jesus is referring to when he declared over and over that one must "believe in Him" to be saved. It is important to note that the cults do not believe in the full divinity of Christ; instead, they believe He was an angel, a created god, or someone less than fully God. Christians must include this in their presentations of the gospel which will lead to the saving reaction of belief in His deity.

The Lord has given me the amazing privilege of leading my four children to Christ and then assisting my own grown daughter to lead her daughter (my granddaughter) to Jesus our Lord. The first responsibility the saints have as parents is to raise their children in the discipline and instruction of the Lord (Ephesians 6:4). It means sharing the gospel with them.

As they were growing up, I made two commitments to the Lord. The first was to be an example of what a Christian should be. This did not mean living a perfect life before them which is impossible. Instead, it meant that I would attempt to live righteously and when I made mistakes, I would ask the Lord for forgiveness. Then I would ask forgiveness from whomever I committed the sin against (including them) and start again. I would study the Scriptures and pray in their presence as well as in my own personal time. I would serve the saints in ministry and share the gospel with unbelievers. When things got hectic and I felt I wasn't going to get the time I needed to study the Word and pray, I would yell, "Coffee drive!" The kids would grab favorite toys, coloring books, and games; then, they would jump into the car to drive around the neighborhood while I listened to the audio Bible and prayed afterward.

Second, I committed myself to teaching them the things of the Lord. I am not very good at a specific weekly study and prayer together though we did do this. It was easier for me to establish a simple weekend rule which was that anybody can go on an errand with daddy. Whenever I ran errands, they would all come. Then, I would speak to them about the Lord (Deuteronomy 6:1-6). Whether we were at the mall, a hardware store, or a supermarket, we talked about Jesus as God's Son. This was not every time but consistently. I took them to church regularly so they would hear the teaching of others and have the influence of other Christian children. As soon as they could do anything in the church, I put them to work for the Lord.

They all believed that Jesus was God's Son and received Him as Savior and Lord about the same age. This was not directly instigated by me. During their elementary years, they came to me at different times and told me that they believed Jesus was God's Son and wanted to be a Christian. One happened in the living room, one in our bedroom, one at the beach, and one at the park. When they asked me if they could become Christians, I explained to them that the bad things we all do is against God. It broke His law and when we break

God's law we must be punished forever. Instead of punishing us, God punished His Son because He loved us.

I explained that it would be like a brother saying to his daddy, "Father, will you punish me instead. I have done nothing wrong, but I love my sister and will do it for her." This is what Jesus did on the cross. He took the punishment for our sin. I described how we must be sorry for the bad things we do which is called "sin" and ask Jesus to forgive us and be our Savior. We must believe that he will forgive our sins and take us to heaven with Him when we die. Also, we must believe that Jesus is the only way to heaven.

Then I asserted that we must make Him the boss of our life even above me, their own daddy. We have to be willing to live our life by obeying His Words in the Bible. When I asked, "Do you still want to become a Christian?" Each said, "Yes!" So, I prayed this prayer as they repeated each sentence after me, "Dear God, I am so sorry for my sins." Then I told them to tell Jesus quietly what some of those sins were that they were sorry for. We continued, "Jesus, I believe you are God's Son. I believe you died on the cross and rose from the dead. I know you did this to take the punishment for my sins. I know you are the only way to heaven. Please forgive my sins and become my Savior. Please be the boss [Lord] of my life and help me to follow what you say you want me to do in the Bible. Amen." I would then announce, "You are now a Christian."

Then for the next several years, we would all celebrate their "spiritual birthdays." The children are all grown now and married to Christian spouses, attending church, and serving the Lord. I look forward to seeing perhaps one or two more generations of my family come to Jesus Christ. This would be one of the greatest joys of my life. Through these many experiences, I learned to proclaim the proper message and depend on our sovereign God to do all the rest. This is God's divine plan. Presenting the proper message of salvation cannot ever be overemphasized. The good news of Jesus must be shared in its fullness. This means that we must put some time into the explanation of the gospel. They came to believe that Jesus was God's Son. Will you take the next step to enter heaven? Will you believe He is God's Son?

Chapter 6

Receive Christ as Savior

Jesus Christ is God's Son and the only Savior of the world. To take the next step, you must believe that Jesus died on the cross for your sins and receive Him as only Savior of the world. In Luke 19:10, Jesus Himself said that He had come to save all those who were lost. In Matthew 1:21, an angel of the Lord told Joseph to name the baby that was in Mary's womb "Jesus" because He would save His people from their sins. In Romans 5:8-11, the apostle Paul wrote that Christians were saved by His death on the cross, justified by His blood, reconciled to God, and delivered from the wrath to come.

Paul told the Corinthians he desired only to preach Jesus Christ and Him crucified (1 Corinthians 2:2). The cross spoke of Jesus Christ being the Savior. In Colossians 2:13-15, Paul declared that though believers were dead in their sins, Christ made them alive. Jesus forgave all their trespasses and took all of the ordinances of God which was against them and nailed them to the cross. All of their sins, whether they are in the past, in the present, or in the future, are forgiven in Him.

Yet, this is not enough. You must know and believe that Jesus is not just one of many ways to heaven. He is the only way. He is the only Savior of the world. In 14:6, John writes, "Jesus said to him, 'I am the way, the truth, and the life. No one comes to the Father, except through me." The Lord Jesus clearly explained to his disciples that He was about to go into heaven to prepare a place for them all. When Thomas asked what was the way to get there, Jesus testified that He was the way, truth, and life. Then Jesus pronounced that no one came to the Father, except through Him.

*In Acts 4:12, Peter preached to the Sanhedrin that Christ had the full authority to save. He asserted that there was no other name that men could call upon to be saved. In John 5:23, Jesus explicitly stated that unless He was honored as the Son, no one could honor the Father who sent Him. Jesus Christ is the only Savior of the world. Often, believers are accused of being too narrow in the faith when it was Jesus Himself who claimed to be the narrow way. Christians are to simply repeat what He said. This is what I am doing to you; I am repeating what He directly said about Himself.

Your response to this proclamation of Jesus Christ as only Savior of the world is to receive Him as Savior. The unsaved must believe that Christ died on the cross to pay the penalty for their sins and accept His saving grace by receiving Him. Jesus was crucified between two thieves. One of the thieves came to realize who Jesus was. Hanging on a cross that thief asked Christ to be His Savior. In Luke 23:42, he cried out to Jesus asking Him to remember him when He came into His kingdom. Jesus assured him that very day he would be in paradise. This dying man received Christ that day.

In 2 Timothy 1:10, Paul declares to Timothy that the one who has abolished death and brought life and immortality through the gospel was "our Savior Jesus Christ." Notice, he uses the possessive pronoun "our" to refer to the Lord being ours. That is a relationship word. The same phrase can be found in 2 Peter 1:1. In that passage, Peter refers to Jesus as "our God and Savior." The acceptance of His saving work is implied in the term "our Savior." This is why in recent years Christians speak of "accepting Christ as Savior."

John clarifies this concept using the term "received." The proper biblical term for one's relationship with Jesus Christ is "received." I always identify myself as having "received Jesus Christ as Savior and Lord." In John 1:12, the apostle refers to our relationship with Jesus Christ in these words, "But as many as received him, to them he gave the right to become God's children, to those who believe in his name." The Greek word translated "receive" means "to take." In the context of a person, it refers to taking with the hand, laying hold of any person or thing in order to use it, to make it one's own, or to give access to oneself in a person-to-person relationship. It is a relationship word.

In John 6:21, this key term was used physically when John described the disciples allowing Christ to enter their boat. They saw the Lord Jesus walking upon the water and were frightened because they thought He was a ghost. When He had convinced them otherwise, they received Jesus into the boat. When He entered, they were immediately at the shore. The Greek word is used spiritually of receiving Christ into people's lives and allowing Him to do His work through His Spirit. As they received Him into the boat, unbelievers are to receive Him into their lives.

In John 19:27, while on the cross, Jesus asked John to care for His mother. John records that she was received into his household from that day forward. Mary became a part of his family. She entered into an intimate, familial relationship with him. In the same way, when Christ is received by one, he enters into a familial relationship (children of God) with Him.

In John 20:22, when the Lord foretold the coming of His Spirit to the disciples, He portrayed it as "receiving" the Holy Spirit. When the Holy Spirit comes into the life of believers at salvation, He is literally received into their bodies (1 John 2:27). They become temples of the Holy Spirit (1 Corinthians 3:16; 6:19). Christ in His Spirit becomes the most important person in their lives and changes them (2 Corinthians 5:17). When Christ is proclaimed as the only Savior, unbelievers must come to Him, recognize His saving work on the cross for them, acknowledge that He is the only way, and receive Him as the Savior accepting His free gift of eternal life.

Early on in my ministry as a Christian Pastoral Counselor, I made a commitment to the Lord that I would present the gospel with everyone that came into my office or confirm their faith. How can someone change without the power of the Spirit? Why solve temporal problems on this Earth and not solve the eternal problems? There is another distinction which is important. Since I practice "Christian" counseling, this involves principles from the Scriptures.

Since the Bible makes distinctions between Christians and non-Christians and even provides different expectations and techniques for each, I need to know whether counselees are or at least they consider themselves to be believers or non-believers. Sometimes, this can lead to some awkwardness in situations when people are not sure of their own salvation or the salvation of their children whom I may be counseling. Whenever this occurs, I utilize a simple strategy to assist in sharing the gospel.

I have the wonderful opportunity of dealing with all ages of people facing all kinds of issues in their lives. Over the course of weeks, I had been working with a couple who had faced some serious marriage problems. They had overcome these major difficulties and were growing rapidly in Christ and in their relationship together. Unfortunately, during the time that the two of them were having these problems, their triplets (two boys and a girl) were acting out in school, not getting along with each other, and defying their parents.

Once the couple was on the right track, it became time to help their children do the same. I asked the parents if the children had received Christ and they said that they were not sure. I asked if anyone else would have shared Christ with them and they did not think so. They had brought them to church intermittently, but not one of them had ever even mentioned Jesus Christ. I explained to them that counseling their children would involve sharing the gospel with them and providing an opportunity for them to receive Christ as Savior and Lord. They gave me permission and I scheduled a meeting with the three of them together. I wanted to see the dynamics of their interaction together before I met with them separately. This was a time of great commotion, much chaos, constant vying for attention, and an unwillingness to listen.

I introduced myself and then provided some background about myself that I thought they could relate to. After this, I described what our individual times together would look like. When I met with them individually, my simple strategy came into play. Rather than force the issue, I simply asked each of them, "Since I am a Christian counselor, I normally give advice from the Scriptures. It provides help differently for Christians and non-Christians, so it is crucial that I know which you are so I can counsel you. Would you like me to counsel you as a Christian or as a non-Christian?" Michael responded, "Yeah, I guess so." His brother, Patrick asserted, "Absolutely, I love Jesus." His sister, Cindy said, "I don't know if I am a Christian or not."

This allowed me to individualize my gospel presentation to each. With Michael, I asked him to explain what he meant by "guessing so." With Patrick, I asked him if he could tell me who he thought Jesus was and how he loved Jesus. With Cindy, I began with the definition of what it means to be a Christian and then asked her if she thought she was a believer. It turned out that not one of the three were true believers. When I asked each of them if they had wanted to receive Jesus Christ that very day and know for sure that they had eternal life with Him, all of them told me they did. I shared the gospel and they all received Christ as Savior and

Lord. They now had the power from the Holy Spirit in their lives and a real commitment to follow His commandments. As a result, I was able to place them on a new Christian track of honoring and glorifying Him at home, school, and church. Of course, this did not happen overnight. Would you like to receive Jesus Christ as Savior right now as these three young people did?

Chapter 7

Submit to Christ as Lord

The next step one must take to enter heaven is to submit to Jesus as Lord. This speaks of Christ's authority in relation to believers. People are to enter into a covenant of obedience to Jesus. Christ is not only the Savior but also the Lord. It is important to note that the key word referring to Jesus in the New Testament is "Lord," and it literally means "master." In Matthew 3:3, Matthew, the author, describes John the Baptist as preparing the way for "the Lord." In Matthew 7:20, Jesus refers to Himself as Lord.

In Matthew 28:18, before Jesus ascended into heaven, He declared, "All authority has been given to me in heaven and on Earth." This refers to His Lordship over all things. In Colossians 1:16, Paul powerfully proclaims it this way, "For by him all things were created, in the heavens and on the Earth, things visible and things invisible, whether thrones or dominions or principalities or powers; all things have been created through him, and for him." Lord Jesus is the ultimate authority over creation.

There are numerous passages in the New Testament in which the Lord Jesus not only declared but demonstrated His full authority over nature (John 6:16-21; Mark 11:12-20), sin (Mark 2:5; Luke 7:49), disease (Matthew 4:23-24; Luke 6:17-19), angels (Hebrews 1:4,6,13), demons (Matthew 8:16), even physical death (John 11:17-44; Luke 7:14), and the church (Colossians 1:18; Romans 8:29). The Lordship of Jesus is a critical part of your entrance into heaven and cannot be left out. In Acts 2:36, Peter declared that all of Israel needed to know that God had made Jesus both Christ and Lord. Both terms for Christ are used. In Acts 4:33, Luke describes the apostles' proclamation of the gospel. He speaks of them witnessing to the resurrection of the "Lord." Jesus is declared the Lord.

In Acts 11:20, witnessing is termed "preaching the Lord Jesus." Luke writes, "But there were some of them, men of Cyprus and Cyrene, who, when they had come to Antioch, spoke to the Hellenists, preaching the Lord Jesus." In Acts 13:12, the gospel is also called the preaching of the Lord. In Ephesians 1:20-23, Paul asserts that Christ is the Lord of all. He is the only one with the authority to save, judge, and rule forever. Jesus Christ is the only one with the right to demand allegiance and command obedience. This is an important element of the gospel because it produces the obedience that is the foundation of the true Christian life.

In James 2:17, the brother of Jesus declared that true faith without works is dead, being by itself. Faith always brings forth obedience. Jesus told his followers that the proof of a saint's true discipleship would be the bearing of much fruit (John 15:8) and would be the natural result of their love for Him (John 14:23). John the Baptist told his audience to bring forth fruit in keeping with their true repentance (Matthew 3:8). Fruit proves this true repentance. The Lordship of Jesus must be declared to bring forth not only true repentance but our obedience.

What then should be your response to this proclamation of Christ as Lord? It is the belief in and recognition of His Lordship. To become a Christian, you must turn your whole life over to a new master. You must relinquish the control of your own life and submit to Him as Master as you attempt to grow in your obedience to Him. This is what Jesus really meant when He claimed one must lose his life to gain it. One must give up his self-directed life for a new one. In Matthew

10:39, Jesus declared, "He who seeks his life will lose it; and he who loses his life for my sake will find it."

This is not a complete and absolute obedience, for this is impossible in this life. It is the desire to obey as best we can. It begins at salvation with submission to His Lordship. In Romans 8:22, Paul describes the groaning that all Christians have within themselves for the redemption of their bodies. At the end, Christians are given a new body without sin and will find absolute submission and obedience. It will not be fully experienced in this life.

The flesh, which is contained in what Paul called the body of death, battles the believer's new man day by day (Romans 7; Ephesians 4:22-23). It is instead the desire and striving after submission and obedience that is found in Romans 12:1-2. True Christians strive after presenting their bodies every single day as living sacrifices, holy, and acceptable to God in service to Him. They endeavor to not be conformed to this world but be transformed by the renewing of their minds and be pleasing to God. This results in what John calls practicing righteousness in his first letter (1 John 2:29). Do not worry; this cannot be done without divine help through God's Holy Spirit which He pours out.

In 1 John 3:5-10, he goes further by stating that one who is born of God, does not continually commit sin. The verb is in the present tense signaling continuous action in present time. One who commits sins (continuous action in present time) is of the Devil. The key concept is continuous action as a pattern of life. Christians sin as individual acts but do not practice sin. They may have difficulty obeying their Lord on every occasion, but as a pattern of life, obedience is present.

True Christians recognize that Jesus Christ is their Lord. This will pour forth into obedience to His commandments. In

Matthew 16:24, Jesus indicated to His disciples that they needed to deny themselves, take up their crosses, and follow Him, if they wanted to come after Him. When Paul recounts his personal testimony in Acts 22:6-10, he was struck down and asked, "What shall I do, Lord?" This was the recognition that Jesus Christ, to whom he was speaking, was Lord and demanded obedience from that moment onward. When we receive Christ, the submission and intent to obey pours forth into salvation. If that submission and intent is real, then the fruit of obedience and good works will demonstrate our true faith. Faith will be shown by works (James 2:14).

In Acts 16, Paul and Silas were singing and praising the Lord in that prison. A powerful Earthquake occurred, and the jailer thought everyone had escaped. Since the jailer would have been killed for this, he prepared to commit suicide. Luke describes, "And brought them out and said, 'Sirs, what must I do to be saved?' They said, 'Believe in the Lord Jesus Christ, and you will be saved, you and your household.'" Paul shouted for him to stop; they were all still there. Awestruck, the jailer responded. Luke describes it. Paul's answer in verse 31 was clear; he needed to believe in the Lord Jesus Christ. The jailer must believe in the Master Jesus Christ. This implies submission and obedience. In Romans 10:9, Paul told the Romans that if they confessed with their mouths that Jesus is Lord and believed in their hearts that He had risen from the dead they would be saved. His Lordship is essential. It must never be omitted from presentations. Obedience is required from the first days of following Christ.

Some would like to separate the Lordship of Christ from His saving work. This is impossible. Can one be saved and produce no fruits? Some desire this separation due to loved ones who claimed to know Jesus but never lived for Him. Unfortunately, there is not one example of this in the New Testament. The thief on the cross never had an opportunity to live for Christ. Yet, in the moments the thief did have, he declared that Jesus was sinless and rebuked the other thief for taunting Him! This was the only good work he could do, and he did do it. Jesus as the Lord demands submission and obedience issuing forth in good works, even on a cross.

Those saved on their death bed will experience the same, even if only for moments or hours. Anyone who has truly repented of sin, turned the other way, and now has the opportunity to live for Christ will produce fruits. Why? They understand that He is the Lord! In Matthew 20:1-16, the Lord told a parable about day laborers who were hired to work in the field at different times of the day and each received the same wage. Every one of them, including the ones hired just before the day was over, worked in the field. This was a picture of salvation. All produced works, once hired, some more, some less. The full understanding of who Jesus is issues forth in submission and obedience to Him as Lord. Once people believe and encounter the deity, majesty, glory, and power of Jesus, they fall on their face in obedience.

One of the ministries I enjoyed when I was a bit younger was as a camp speaker for junior high and high school at winter and summer Christian camps. I remember these big church buses rolling in on a Saturday afternoon to stay for a whole week of teaching, activities, and relaxation. I would preach Saturday night, Sunday morning, Sunday evening, and then every single morning and evening until they left the following Saturday. It was a very exciting and yet very tense time speaking to about two hundred young people that much. I spent much time praying for boldness, wisdom, and clarity of speech.

I remember as soon as this camp was over that week, I would begin praying every single day for the next year those busses would come rolling in again. So, for one whole year, I would pray every day for the salvation of every young person or for each one's growth in Christ, even though I did not even know their names yet. As a result, I saw God do amazing things at those camps. One time, about mid-week, I had been speaking on the great difference between being a member of a church or attending youth group and being a Christian with a personal relationship to Jesus Christ.

After the talk, as the teens were leaving the amphitheater, two young ladies approached me. One of them, whose name was Kim, said very straightforwardly, "Hi Pastor Don (my title in those days), I am a Catholic, am I saved?" Wow, that was a powerful question. I prayed to the Lord for wisdom. I looked at her and replied, "It doesn't matter whether you are Catholic, Presbyterian, Methodist, Baptist, or a member of any other religious group, you must have a personal, saving relationship with the Lord Jesus Christ just as I have been speaking about for the last several days? Do you have this kind of relationship with Him?"

The second girl silently standing next to her friend looked shocked. Kim thought for a moment and said, "No, I don't think so. I know who He is, but I have never asked Him to be my Savior or submitted to Him as Lord." I looked at the other young lady, whose name was Angie, and asked her, "Do you?" And she replied, "Yes, I really do." Then she smiled. I turned once again to Kim and asked, "Would you like to become a Christian and turn your life over to Jesus as Savior and Lord right now?"

The young lady looked at me in deep thought and then said solemnly, "Yes, I would." Angie's face turned white, like a ghost. As I led her friend Kim into the kingdom of God, Angie stood there with a stunned look on her face. Then as we prayed a prayer asking for salvation, Angie kept shaking her head in utter disbelief. Afterward, the two were rejoicing together as they walked away. Then Angie turned back and walked over to me and said boldly, "Pastor Don, I have been praying for my friend Kim to become a Christian since I was a little girl. Now I was able to see God answer my prayer right before my eyes. This was awesome!" I replied, "I have been praying for your friend for a year, and I got to watch God answer my prayer right before my eyes also. That's awesome too!" Wow! What joy and amazement we had that day as Kim turned her life over to Jesus! Will you turn your life over to Him? Will you submit yourself to Him right now?

FINDING THE LIGHT

Chapter 8

Affirm Christ's Resurrection

As I present to you the good news, I want to take a few minutes to present the evidence for the deity of Christ. To prove His divinity Jesus did many miracles, fulfilled many prophecies (both Old Testament and His own), and rose from the dead. Of course, His resurrection from death itself was his greatest miracle and fulfillment of prophecy. How could anything be greater than rising from the dead?

I do not want you to base your beliefs on merely what I say. God wants His evidence presented so the Holy Spirit can use it to work in your heart. Your entrance into heaven cannot be based on some inspirational experience or feelings but on the historical facts. The Lord God spent years creating this evidence and wants it to be declared to you. Also, this affirmation can be referred to when doubt comes not some emotional feeling.

First, Jesus performed numerous miracles as He preached the kingdom to confirm who He was. In Matthew 4:23, the apostle records that the Lord proclaimed the gospel and then healed the sick. This was His usual method of evangelism. The Lord would proclaim His deity and prove it through miracles. In Matthew 11:4-6, when John the Baptist sent his followers to inquire as to Christ's deity, Jesus spoke of the miracles that He performed: He healed the sick, made the lame walk, the blind to see, the deaf to hear, and the mute to speak. In John 5:36, the Lord challenged the Jewish people to consider the works (miracles) He had done as a testimony to His deity. He never appealed to some inner experience they should have had. He never asked them if how they felt.

Second, Jesus fulfilled numerous prophecies in order to demonstrate that He was the Son of God. So, the world would be able to identify God's Son in human flesh, He provided many signs or prophecies through the prophets of Israel. Over many years, a variety of them would speak of God's judgment on Israel and then encourage His people by foretelling His future blessing through the sending of His Son and their Messiah (Anointed One). Jesus fulfilled most of the Old Testament prophecies about Him through God's providence (Micah 5:2; Psalm 72:10; Jeremiah 31:15; Hosea 11:1; Isaiah 9:1-2). Others, Christ fulfilled intentionally and deliberately (Luke 4:21; John 2:22; 13:18; 17:12; 19:28). Then He Himself also predicted events that would occur that were fulfilled in His final week of life (Matthew 26:1-2, 6-12; John 3:14-15; 8:28-29; 12:23-24).

Third, Jesus resurrected from the dead to demonstrate His deity. This fulfilled many prophecies and proved His deity. His resurrection was predicted in the Old Testament (Job 19:25-26; Psalm 16:8-11; 22:19-24; Isaiah 53:10-11) and it was fulfilled with evidence in the New Testament (1 Corinthians 15:5-11; Matthew 28:9-10). Luke begins Acts by stating that the Lord appeared to His disciples after His resurrection for a period of forty days and provided many proofs that He was truly alive from the dead (Acts 1:3).

Before His resurrection, Christ proclaimed to the Jewish people that He would fulfill a critical prophecy from their Scriptures which would be a sign for them identifying Him as the true Messiah. The prophecy was the sign of Jonah. As Jonah was in the sea creature three days and three nights, so He would be in the Earth three days and three nights. The implication was that as Jonah was spewed onto the sand, so would Christ be spewed from the Earth and rise from the dead (Matthew 12:39-40; 16:4; Luke 11:29). This was such an important element in His gospel message.

On other occasions, He predicted His own resurrection. Jesus declared that if they destroyed the temple, He would rebuild it in three days. Jesus was referring to His death and resurrection. This analogy confounded the Jewish people because they thought the Lord meant their physical temple. Yet, this prediction was often mentioned in His preaching. This is obvious because the prophecy was so well known by the people of Israel.

The knowledge of this prediction about the temple was so widespread, it was used by the false witnesses against Jesus at His trial as words of sedition against the Jews (Matthew 26:61; Mark 14:58). These words were a part of the insults by the people walking by Jesus while He was on the cross. They mentioned this prediction demanding He prove He was the Son of God by coming down from the cross (Matthew 27:39-40; Mark 15:29). John acknowledges that when Christ had risen from the dead, the disciples remembered this prophecy and believed in Him. This was an important element in His message (John 2:18-22).

In Luke 24:25-27, there were two on the road to Emmaus who encountered the risen Christ, but they did not know it. These two men were confused as to who Christ was and the events that had just unfolded in Israel. Jesus rebuked them because they did not believe the prophets and what had just been fulfilled concerning His suffering and resurrection. The chastisement did not happen because they did not know; it occurred because they did not believe. These prophecies were well known in Israel. Then, He explained how Jesus had fulfilled many of the prophecies in the Old Testament. Later, He revealed Himself to clearly to them and they went immediately to His disciples. These two men described what happened and declared that Jesus was indeed alive. This proclamation of fulfilled prophecy and physical proof that He had risen from the dead was important to the Lord.

Not only did Jesus proclaim His deity and demonstrate it through His miracles, His fulfillment of prophecy, and His resurrection, but His disciples were told to proclaim what they had seen in Him. They were commanded to share His message and the proofs of His deity to those in Jerusalem, Judea, Samaria, and all the Earth (Acts 1:8). This is exactly what they did. He told them they would be His "witnesses." They were simply to share what they had seen and heard.

John, the apostle explains this commission by Christ to his readers in 1 John 1:1-2 when he comments, "That which was from the beginning, that which we have heard, that which we have seen with our eyes, that which we saw, and our hands touched, concerning the Word of life (and the life was revealed, and we have seen, and testify, and declare to you the life, the eternal life, which was with the Father, and was revealed to us)."

The disciples heard Christ's message and saw His many miracles and His fulfillment of numerous prophecies. They talked and walked with Him after His resurrection. He gave them many convincing proofs. All of this was experienced by all their senses. They saw Him with their own eyes, heard Him with their own ears, and touched Him with their own hands. Then they merely declared Christ, His message, and these proofs to everyone they encountered. The four gospel writers appealed to the miracles, fulfilled prophecies, and the resurrection of Jesus that confirmed His deity in their written evangelistic gospel messages. These biographies are filled with numerous examples.

Since Christians today are not eyewitnesses, how do we confirm and defend our faith to you? Consider Luke, who also was not an eyewitness. Yet, in Luke 1:1-4, the author explains that he investigated carefully all that had happened from actual eyewitness accounts. This way all who read His gospel would know with certainty that Christ was the Son of God. Now, I am declaring these to you!

Your response to the defense of the deity of Jesus should be the firm belief that Christ is the Son of God (deity) from the miracles, fulfilled prophecies, and His resurrection from the dead. The biblical response to this is an affirmation of the resurrection. In Romans 10:9, Paul explains, "That if you will confess with your mouth that Jesus is Lord and believe in your heart that God raised him from the dead, you will be saved." Paul said that if one confesses that Jesus is Lord with His mouth and believes He rose from the dead in his heart, he will be saved. In 1 Corinthians 15, Paul gives the essence of the gospel which is Christ died, was buried, and rose again according to the Scriptures (verses 3-4).

In John 20:24-30, Thomas, His disciple, refused to believe in the resurrection of Christ until he witnessed the wounds on His hands and put his finger in His side. Eight days later, Jesus appeared and allowed Thomas to verify this miracle with His own senses. Immediately, he declared that Jesus was "my Lord and my God." Notice the possessive pronoun. He was declaring his own salvation from the recognition of Christ's resurrection which proved His deity.

Then Jesus paints a portrait of believers in the future, who will never witness the wounds. These beloved saints will be blessed because though they will not have seen, yet they will believe in His resurrection. This describes all those who have come to Christ after His ascension, except Paul. Remember from our earlier discussion. This belief comes through the power of the Holy Spirit working in your heart as I have presented the evidence to you.

When I came to Jesus Christ, I wanted the tools necessary to share and prove my faith. I was on a big college campus where the students were debating many philosophies and ways of looking at life; I wanted to get into the game. I loved the intellectual stimulation of investigation, research, and discussion. I had joined a campus group of Christians who were extremely evangelistic. They had set a table up in the center of campus and many of us manned the table. They discussed Jesus with those passing by. This was a great time of anticipation, fear, and joy as God used us to share His good news with these many college students.

We had heard that a new book had been published with the proofs for the veracity of the Bible and the Sonship of Jesus Christ. It explained in detail the fulfilled prophecies, miracles, and proofs for the resurrection of Jesus Christ. This was exactly where my interests were. I was so thrilled and desirous of this book that I drove up to the author's office to get one of the first copies. With that in hand, as soon as the new semester registration began, I registered for my very first speech class. I was so excited to present these proofs that I determined that I would do it for one of my speeches.

Finally, a speech came where we had to use visuals, so I developed a series of slides on the numerous proofs for the resurrection of Jesus Christ. I did not want to see my fellow students perish in their sins, so I mustered up the courage to share my faith. When it eventually came my turn, I took them progressively through the verification of the Lord's death.

I had slides which discussed the blood and water pouring out of his side, the lack of need to break His legs to suffocate him because He was already dead, the ritualistic Jewish burial with the oils, perfumes, and tightly wound bandages, the known location of the tomb, the massive rock that was placed in front of it, the sealing of it with Rome's insignia, and the placing of the guards before it.

Then I discussed the empty tomb of Jesus, the bandages lying flat with the head piece rolled up, the removal of the stone, the breaking of the official seal, the passing out of the guards, and the angelic presence when the first witnesses arrived. After this, I shared with the class the testimony of each and every witness to the resurrected Christ. I was so excited, enthusiastic, and committed. I wanted everyone to believe and receive Jesus Christ as Savior and Lord. I even gave an invitation to invite Christ into their lives after class with me. I suggested that they talk to me if they have some questions or wanted to dialogue about Him.

After the presentation, the instructor complemented me on my skills and preparation as a speaker. Then he casually mentioned that he probably would have considered picking a different topic, but it was certainly my choice. Everyone just sat there in silence. After several more speeches the class was finally over. As I was walking out of the room figuring that nothing had happened, I felt a tap on my right shoulder. This young man behind me quietly mumbled, "Can I talk to you?" I agreed and Dennis and I went for coffee at one of the college cafes. I admit that I was nervous, but I knew the Lord would work His will in this situation.

He began to describe how depressed he had been since he started college. Everything seemed simple and clear in high school, but everything he valued was now questioned and he felt there was no place to land. He knew that if he landed on a man-made philosophy, it would eventually crumble. When I shared the Lord Jesus Christ and the solid evidence and power of His death and resurrection, he told himself, "This Jesus was more than a man and this book was more than a philosophy book. This was the truth."

Then he asked me to please help him receive Jesus Christ as Savior and Lord. He wanted a relationship with the living

Christ and His father through His Spirit. Right there, in that cafe at a major university I had the privilege of bringing him to Christ. Will you acknowledge His miracles? Will you also believe in His fulfilled prophecies? Will you affirm His real resurrection from the dead? Will you take the next step to enter God's heaven?

Chapter 9

Love Christ in a Relationship

Christ isn't simply an historical man of the past, nor is He a distant God of the present but the God-Man, risen, alive, and desirous of a real relationship with people. The essence of Christianity is not just obeying a list of precepts but, more importantly, following a person in a relationship with Him. Though the Scriptures do not utilize the word relationship, it assumes it. John distinctly said in 1 John 5:11-13 that if one has (possesses) the Son, one has (possesses) eternal life. This verb presupposes a relationship.

In Matthew 7:23, Jesus speaks of the Day of Judgment and explains that some will call Him Lord and expect Him to usher them into heaven. Instead, He will send them into hell because He never "knew" them. The word "know" in that passage means an experiential knowledge which is more than intellectual. The Septuagint uses this key Greek term to characterize the intimacy between a man and woman. It is a relational knowing. Here is the key concept. People know of many historical figures, but they do not have a relationship of love, faith, and obedience with them. Some grow up with some knowledge of Jesus but do not trust Him as Savior or obey Him as the Lord. They know only "of Him." Christians know Him.

In Revelation, Jesus discusses His relationship with two churches. In Revelation 2:4, the Lord accuses the church at Ephesus of departing from their first love. Their motivation in their persistence and endurance was no longer love for Him. True Christians are in love with Jesus Christ. This is an authentic relationship. In Revelation 3:16, Jesus charges the church in Laodicea with being lukewarm. They were neither hot nor cold toward Him. In verse 20, He offers those in the church a relationship with Him when he proclaims that He is standing at the door and knocking. If people in the church "hear" His voice and "open" the door, Christ will "dine" with them. These are relationship words.

In 1 John 1:3, John indicates that he proclaimed the gospel to them so they could fellowship with the Lord Jesus Christ. He describes it in this way, "That which we have seen and heard we declare to you, that you also may have fellowship with us. Yes, and our fellowship is with the Father, and with his Son, Jesus Christ." The word "fellowship" speaks of a relationship. It means participation in a partnership. This is what you must do to be saved. You enter into a partnership with Christ and participate in the plan of your Lord and Master. This does not refer to working your way into God's grace in order to enter heaven. It simply refers to the fact that Christians realize and acknowledge that they are in a love relationship with a living God, not a dead prophet.

In Matthew 22:37, when the Lord was asked what was the greatest commandment, He declared that it was to love God with all of one's heart, soul, and mind. This was a perfect description of a meaningful and robust relationship. One's response to the proclamation of a relationship with Christ is to love Him. The word love used of Christ in the Greek in its most basic understanding is to value or to prize. It does not convey the feelings implied by the English word. Feelings may be part of it but does not compose the central aspect. The key is this valuing and prizing of someone or something which issues forth in a variety of loving words and actions.

John delineates these critical fundamental elements when he describes exactly how to love the brethren in 1 John 3:18. He asserts that they are to love in deed and in truth as well as in their words and language. To love someone must by its nature be expressed. Those expressions are found in both verbal and physical actions with loving language and deeds according to the truth. The truth here refers to the Scripture. Loving someone is always according to God's Word.

In the case of Christ, for you to come to Him, you must believe that He is the God of the universe, has died for you, will forgive your sins, submit to Him as Lord, and love Him for it. Then you and I spend our lives learning about Him through His Word, speaking and talking to Him through prayer, and loving Him through obedience and good deeds. We love Him the way the Bible tells us to love Him. The way He desires to be loved. This love is the light into heaven.

In John 14:15, Jesus declares that if someone loves Him, he will keep His commandments. Then in verse 24, the Lord pronounced that someone who does not love Him does not keep His commandments. Obedience flows out of love. In John 14:23, just before this declaration, John recorded this statement from the Lord, "Jesus answered him, 'If a man loves me, he will keep my word. My Father will love him, and we will come to him, and make our home with him.'"

After this, Jesus makes the most amazing statement that if someone loves Him, the Father will love them. Also, if one loves the Son, then one loves His Father, the true God. In John 17:26, Christ professes that the love that a Christian has for Him (Jesus) is in reality the love of the Father for Jesus in them. Continually, the writers of the New Testament explain Christians are those who love Jesus Christ.

In Ephesians 6:24, Paul closes his letter with a blessing of grace that addresses all his believing readers as those who love the Lord Jesus Christ. In 1 Corinthians 16:22, Paul concludes his letter by pronouncing a curse on all who will not love the Lord Jesus Christ. Here he is generally speaking of all unbelievers but also alluding to the false prophets that were disrupting the Corinthian church and were standing against him. They will spend an eternity in hell and without God.

In James 1:12, the half-brother of Jesus promises a reward to all the Christians who persevere under trial. He addresses them as "those who love Him." Later in chapter 2, verse 5, the head of the Jerusalem church contrasts the poor of this world with the rich. He discloses a promise to the poor who are believers. The Lord promised that those who love Him will be rich in faith and heirs of the kingdom. Once again, he addresses believers as the ones who love the Lord.

In 1 Peter 1:8, Peter complements his readers concerning their love for Christ. He characterizes them as those who are filled with joy. Why? Though they have not seen Him, they love Him! He portrays true believers as those who believe in Jesus Christ as God and love their Lord. This was a lesson that the apostle learned the hard way! When Jesus restored Peter to ministry after his denial, Jesus questioned his love for Him (John 21:16-17). Why? Love for Christ is the core of one's salvation.

This love for Christ will be in direct opposition to the love of the world. When an unbeliever repents, he forsakes the love of the world and replaces it with a love for Christ. The world would be the society of unbelievers with everything that is evil within it. John describes it in 1 John 2:15-16. The world is comprised of the lust of the eyes, the flesh, and pride of living. This would be whatever the eyes and flesh passionately desire and whatever will cause unbelievers to boast concerning the way in which they live. This does not mean you stop living in or enjoying the "good and holy" things the world offers.

In James 4:1-10, James stands against all those who seek their own pleasure above God among his readers. This led to fighting and quarreling among themselves. He exclaims that friendship with the world is enmity against their God. These seekers of pleasure wanted all that the world offered and James identifies them as spiritual adulterers. He uses the Old Testament concept of Israel's idolatry as adulterating their love relationship with God (Ezekiel 16:15-19, 30; Hosea 1:2). Their love of the world and its pleasures was the same kind of adultery. Christians view the Hebrew people as sinning in a way they would never do; yet often do the same thing.

This adulterous love can take a variety of forms: the love of men's approval (John 12:43), the love of money (1 Timothy 6:10), the love of self (2 Timothy 3:2), the love of pleasure (2 Timothy 3:4), the love of this present world (2 Timothy 4:10), the love of the wages of unrighteousness (2 Peter 2:15), and the love of preeminence (3 John 1:9).

Why? Why must someone turn from loving this world to loving God instead? The answer comes from the parable of the seed thrown among the thorns in Matthew 13:22. The love of the world (the deceitfulness of riches and its worries) choke the Word and they fall away, never allowing the seed of faith to take root. Jesus clarifies this struggle between two loves when He speaks of those serving two masters in Matthew 6:24. Either they will love one and hate the other or be devoted to one or despise the other. People cannot love God and love money (the essence of the world system). They are naturally and supernaturally opposed to each other.

This does not mean that true believers will not struggle with the flesh. They will, but they will also regularly win the battle. In Romans 7:18-20, the apostle claims he desires good, but sometimes does evil. He battles his flesh (sin principle in the body) within his mind. In Galatians 5:17, Paul indicates that the Spirit in Christians will oppose the flesh in them so they will not do what they want. Here lies the key point. A true believer will desire to be righteous through the Spirit in Him, but his body will desire to be evil. As the daily battles are fought, the believer will regularly choose good, but the unbeliever will choose evil.

This love for Him is deeper than human love. There are those who may have the feeling of love for Christ, being stirred anew with penetrating music, funny and appealing sermons, colorful lighting, a dramatic stage, standing with many others who feel the same, attending a huge service, and being enveloped with surround sound, yet are not saved. Feelings are never enough. If people only have the feelings of love for Jesus Christ, they will discover that those feelings fade. Then, they will be off to the next feeling of love in another religion. All human feelings go up and down, but true faith and real love remain for a lifetime. This is why the marriage covenant is also for a lifetime (Ephesians 5:32). This love is not based on feeling but based on faith.

One Saturday night, I was at a get together at a friend's house and we were all sitting in the living room talking with one another. Suddenly, I realized it was getting late and I checked my watch and discovered that it was 10:30pm. I stood up and thanked the host for a great evening and then explained to the group that I had to get up early the next morning and so I had to depart. Suddenly a voice rang out, "What could you possibly be doing so early in the morning and so important that you have to leave now?" I glanced over in the direction of the voice, and it was a co-worker of mine named Brian. I indicated that I had to go to church to teach a bible class the next morning that began at 8:00am and wanted to get a decent night's sleep. I explained to him how important it was for me to sleep at least eight hours so I would be at my best the next day.

Brian responded with a chastising, "The Bible! You know, there are many other good religious books beside the Bible. I consider myself a seeker of truth and have studied all the major religions and picked out the best of each. I follow my own religion." Though I really desired a good night's sleep, I couldn't let this one go by. I asked him if he had actually read the Bible. Brian explained that he had not read the Bible or actually any of the other religious books, but he had read several books about the major religions of the world.

I issued him this challenge, "If you are a real seeker of the truth, then I dare you to read the Bible and compare it to the other religious writings. I dare you to compare any religion to a relationship with Jesus Christ. Read them all. If you are a seeker of truth and your heart is open to it, then you will see that the Bible is the truth, and that Jesus is real and alive!" He laughed uproariously. Then he declared, "Okay, I will take that challenge and return a challenge. You get me a Bible, be available to answer questions and I will read it first. Then I will read the others."

I wrote down his address and took a Bible over to him the next day. I suggested that he begin with the Gospel of John because I wanted Him to meet Jesus and walk with Him down the dusty roads of Palestine. I wanted Him to see what a relationship would mean. All the other religious leaders and prophets are dead, but Jesus is alive. He agreed with my proposal, and I gave him my number telling him to call anytime with his questions. Over the next three months, he read, and I answered questions about the Scriptures, Jesus and this love relationship.

He became enthralled with the Lord Jesus Christ. After Brian read the Gospel of John, he proceeded through the other gospels. During those months, I shared the gospel with him several times and asked him if he desired to receive Jesus

Christ. He responded with, "No, you said I should compare the books and that is what I am going to do."

Slowly he accumulated other religious writings including the Koran, the Book of Mormon, The Gospel of Thomas, the Lost Books of the Bible, the Catholic Catechism, the Talmud, and the various "holy writings" of Hinduism, Buddhism, Taoism, and Confucianism. Then he told me he thought I should read the writings with him and see if I was wrong. I took the challenge and we read and read. It was a long and arduous journey, but I knew the Bible and Jesus could stand up to any challenge or book. Finally, we finished, and he said to me now I am going to take some time to process all of this in my mind because I really do want the truth.

Two weeks later, Brian called me and asked me to come right over. When I arrived, he asked me to come in and sit down. He looked me straight in the eyes and said, "Thank you so much for taking this long and difficult journey with me." He held up the Bible and declared, "This book is true, and I am ready to receive Christ as my Savior and Lord. No one is like Jesus, and I want a relationship with Him." That day his life and eternity were changed forever. He now issues the very same challenge I issued to him to every unbeliever he meets. Do you desire that relationship? Will you make a serious commitment to love Jesus? To love Him will be the path to heaven.

Chapter 10

Depend on Faith Alone

Salvation is by faith alone, not by good works. This is another critical truth you must believe. People cannot work their way into God's heaven. Good works are always a result of salvation. Over and over, the Lord Jesus Christ declared that one must believe in Him to be saved. In John 3:16, Jesus told Nicodemus, "For God so loved the world, that he gave his one and only Son, that whoever believes in him should not perish, but have eternal life." He claimed that whosoever believes in Him will have eternal life.

In John 4:39, John describes the salvation of a group of people, who had been brought to the well by the Samaritan woman, as believing in Him. In John 6:29, Jesus told His listeners that they must believe in Him who God sent. In John 6:35, Jesus declared that He was the bread of life, and they must believe in Him for eternal life. There are many Bible passages which teach this simple yet very powerful truth.

The apostles claimed that belief was the essential element, not works. In Acts 4:4, Luke describes those who were saved as those who had believed. In Acts 5:14, Luke declares that multitudes had believed. In Acts 8:37, when the eunuch from Ethiopia heard the gospel, he confessed that he believed that Jesus Christ was the Son of God. Peter preached to Cornelius that anyone who believes in Christ receives forgiveness of sins. In Acts 16:36, Paul told the Philippian jailer and all in his household that they must believe in the Lord Jesus Christ to be saved. Belief in Jesus alone was constantly proclaimed. Over and over Jesus declared belief without works to save.

The Lord Jesus spoke often concerning the producing of fruit in keeping with true faith. Good works are the result of faith. In Matthew 13:23, the Lord compared believers to good seeds that always produce the fruit of righteous deeds by their faith. In John 15:2, Jesus compares Himself to a vine and His true followers as those branches which produce fruit. If His branches abide in Him, they will bear much fruit because apart from Him they can do nothing (John 15:5).

This is different than submission to Christ as Lord. The submission to Jesus as Lord is the saving response and our obedience is the result. There has been some controversy concerning whether one is saved if one believes but does not submit. Some desire to make distinctions in their minds to allow some they love into the kingdom who profess Christ but have never lived differently or even attempted righteous living. True believers always behave like true believers with good works. The amount of good works may vary, but there are always faith-based works. When I say, "good works," I mean practicing righteousness in every area of life. If one falls away and begins to behave like they do not know the Lord, then we should expect the Lord God to discipline His child back into obedience (Hebrews 12:4-11). True believers receive discipline and training from their Lord as a Father assists his children.

To be saved, unbelievers must believe that faith alone will save them. They must trust in Christ's saving work on the cross alone rather than the accumulation of good works or personal righteousness. In Romans 3:28, Paul declares that Christians are justified by faith apart from the works of the Law. Once again, in Romans 5:1, he asserts that believers are justified by faith alone. When false teachers fooled the Galatians into thinking that Gentiles had to be circumcised, Paul explained to them that the works of the law could not justify but only hearing by faith (Galatians 2:16). Men can only be justified (declared righteous) by faith in what Christ did for them on the cross.

In Ephesians 2:8, Paul clearly explains that salvation is a result of faith, not works. Why? So, no man can boast before God. No one will ever be able to claim that he worked his way into heaven. Instead, as has been seen, good works pour forth from a life of faith. In Ephesians 2:10, Paul continues his discussion by indicating that once faith comes Christians are to walk in good works. In Colossians 1:10, Paul prays that the church would walk in a worthy manner, pleasing God in everything, and producing fruit in every good work. In 2 Timothy 6:18, Paul encourages Timothy to instruct the saints, who are well-to-do, to become rich in good works. Righteous works flow supernaturally from true faith, they do not save. This is an important distinction.

I became a Christian many years ago at the University of Southern California. I'll never forget that day. I thought I was so important because I had an academic scholarship to USC. I was young and excited, thinking I had the whole world in front of me. In fact, when I looked into my future, I saw everything I could ever want: power, prestige, fame, money, happiness, and fulfillment. On October third of my sophomore year, I found myself wondering around the campus of USC at lunch time. I was doing what I normally did at this time which was looking for a place to sit and eat my brown bag lunch. Often, different campus groups would sponsor speakers to come and address the students at lunch time.

So, I had about an hour and a half between classes to find something to do. While I was eating a sandwich in one hand and munching on a bag of chips in the other, I walked by an auditorium on campus and saw a sign that said, "How To Have a Fulfilling Marriage." I figured, since I was planning on becoming a psychologist, I should know something about marriage, so in I walked. There were almost 200 students there. After a few moments, an evangelist from a Christian group walked on the stage. Later, he would become a highly prominent writer and speaker in Christian apologetics and evidence for the faith, but at this time, he was just a young guy sharing his faith for a Christian organization on campus.

Scott presented many principles and examples on how to have a fulfilling marriage from his own relationship with his spouse. After about twenty minutes, he explained to the student audience the real reason he and his wife had such an amazing marriage. He declared that it was because they both knew and loved the Lord Jesus Christ. He told the students that he would like to share the gospel with them because he loved them and did not want them to perish. At the time, I thought that was a bit odd. He explained that he did not want to force them to hear the gospel, so they could leave if they wanted.

As a result, numerous students got up and walked out. I had not finished my sandwich or my chips, and it was hot outside, so I stayed with about three other students scattered about the theater. Scott began sharing the gospel of Jesus Christ. He described God's love for me and said the Bible indicated that there was a great chasm between man and God and that chasm was sin. God, being absolutely holy, must judge those sins; no one was exempt. In Romans 3:23, Paul wrote that all had sinned and fallen short of the glory of God. The wages (payment) for those sins would be spiritual death in an eternity of punishment (Romans 6:23).

All of a sudden, I realized that I had already committed a massive number of sins since I was a young child. There was still the possibility of committing a great many more. Right there, the weight of about ninety years of sin came upon me, and I knew there would be no way that any amount of fame, power, prestige, accomplishment, awards, money, or even doing good works in this life could compensate for my sins. There was and would be too many! I could not do enough good works to save myself. Then Scott shared God's holy solution, which was His Son, Jesus Christ. Our God had so loved the world (including you and me) that He had given His only Begotten Son to die on the cross for us (John 3:16).

If we would believe in Him, our sins would be forgiven, and we would be possessors of eternal life with Him. He mentioned that faith in Christ alone would save us and then declared that we could not do enough good works to save ourselves. This was exactly what I had been thinking. After proclaiming the entire gospel, Scott asked if any students would like to stay and receive Jesus Christ as their Savior and Lord. With that question, the other three students got up and walked out. Suddenly, I was left there alone in that large auditorium at lunch time that day and I raised my hand. I wanted desperately to be forgiven. I wanted desperately to have this eternal life.

While Scott was standing on the stage and I was sitting in the chair, I prayed a prayer declaring Jesus Christ to be the Son of God and only Savior of the world. I acknowledged that Jesus had risen from the dead and I relinquished my will and life to Him in obedience as Lord. Afterward, I went up and thanked Scott for releasing me from the burden of working my way to heaven. Christians have the only belief system that teaches this truth. All others are works based. Would you like to be released from that burden of having to work your way into heaven when in reality you cannot?

Chapter 11

Proclaim Christ in Baptism

If you decide to take the light of Jesus Christ and enter heaven, the next important step will be to declare Him your Savior and Lord to the world through water baptism (water immersion). Baptism does not and cannot save you. Yet, God desires new believers to proclaim their new faith in Christ to the world through water baptism. It must become the initial response a believer makes in His obedience to Christ as Lord of his life.

In the New Testament baptism was continually declared and practiced as the initial response after someone became a Christian. One believed and then the person was baptized. This was also the pattern of Jesus Christ and the apostles in their proclamation of the good news. In John 3:22, John, the apostle, records that the Lord Jesus was in the land of Judea baptizing. Obviously, this occurred after the preaching of the kingdom which is always described by the gospel writers as Christ's message of redemption (Matthew 4:17; Mark 1:15; Luke 8:1). They believed and then were baptized. Actually, Jesus was preaching the kingdom, but His disciples were baptizing those who were receiving Him as Savior and Lord (John 4:2). In fact, in Matthew 28:18-20, the risen Lord Jesus commanded His followers to make disciples by going, then baptizing, and finally teaching others.

In Acts 2:41, after the people received Peter's word (the gospel), then they were baptized. They received Jesus Christ (John 1:12), and then were baptized. This would have been a momentous undertaking because more than three thousand people were saved that day. Yet, they baptized every one of them. In Acts 8:12-13, Luke records that once some of the citizens of Samaria were saved, Philip baptized them. Then in Acts 8:35-36, Philip is sent to the Ethiopian eunuch and shared the good news with him. As soon as this high official believed, he asked Philip to be baptized. Luke described it this way, "Philip opened his mouth, and beginning from this Scripture, preached to him Jesus. As they went on the way, they came to some water, and the eunuch said, 'Behold, here is water. What is keeping me from being baptized?'" He knew he must be baptized. How did the eunuch know this? Philip must have explained it during his presentation of the good news.

In Acts 10:47, once Cornelius, the centurion, and his household had received Christ as Savior and Lord, Peter ordered them to be baptized and they were. In Acts 16:15, Lydia and her household believed and were baptized. Then a few verses later in Acts 16:33, the jailer and his household believed and were baptized. In Acts 18:8, Luke described the salvation of Crispus, his household, and many Corinthians. Paul preached the Word and they believed. Then they were baptized. In Acts 22:16, Paul testifies as to how he became a Christian. The apostle describes his baptism by Ananias. As soon as Paul's blindness was removed by the prophet, he demanded that Paul rise and be baptized. In fact, he asked Paul why he was delaying this outward sign of his inward faith. Here is a prophet of God demonstrating that baptism was to immediately occur after faith in Jesus Christ. Baptism follows but does not save.

Then what is baptism, its purpose, and why is it so closely linked to salvation? The Lord Jesus Christ desires for His people to announce their newly obtained salvation to the saints and the world through the outward sign of baptism. Therefore, baptism was to be practiced in public for all to see. The immersion in the water was to signify that they had died to their old lives and been raised to new ones through Christ's death and resurrection (Romans 6:4). Though often the church will baptize in its church building and then invite the world to come in, it is not as close to the biblical pattern as baptizing where all can see. Another important purpose is to have people publicly identify themselves with others in the church, the body of Christ (1 Corinthians 12:13).

Here is the point. Wherever the unsaved travel in the world, they should constantly be viewing new Christians being baptized by other Christians. Everywhere on this Earth from Jerusalem to the outermost parts, those who do not know Christ should be bombarded by the scene of those in the church of Jesus Christ welcoming new converts into their midst again and again. People should see the outward sign of other people being cleansed from sin and becoming brand-new creations. Then those same people should be able to watch the old lives of those being baptized pass away and their new lives come as they live righteously for Him (2 Corinthians 5:17)!

This is exactly what the people in the first century saw and people today should see. Since water baptism should proceed immediately after salvation, some have mistakenly thought it was an actual element of the salvation process. It is not. Of course, the "immediately" doesn't necessarily mean the next minute or day, but it does mean soon after faith. Also, it was always a baptism of true believers. No babies were ever baptized in the Bible. Baptism was invariably by full immersion in physical water.

When an opportunity came to run a vacation bible school for my church (a week-long event of two hours each day for children), I jumped at this opportunity with one stipulation. I asked them to allow me to design the camp around a fresh, current, and biblical theme. For this theme, I decided to use the apostle Paul's analogy of Christians as soldiers at war with the forces of evil. I picked this because the military and police themes were extremely popular in books, television shows, and movies at the time. I also had several police and highway patrol officers in our church that I could recruit to help.

I borrowed a flight uniform from my brother who was a civilian mechanic on an air force base. The first day, we had a CHP officer ride his motorcycle around the parking lot as the children (3rd to 6th graders) arrived. There was a large sign in front of the church that read, "Welcome to SWAT CAMP." Below it in smaller letters were written, "**S**piritual **W**eapons **A**nd **T**actics For Growth In Christ (Ephesians 6:10-19)." It was very exciting for the children.

The day was broken up into four periods. The first was a large group teaching time (Meeting with Our Commander God), the second had a small group application and prayer time (Battle Strategy Session), the third involved a fun game time (Training and Obstacle Course), and the fourth time encouraged a positive interaction with law enforcement personnel who attended our church and were believers (Law Enforcement Interaction). One of our officers always brought a vehicle or some equipment that he could also demonstrate.

The teaching time explained each piece of the armor of God with one element of the gospel message taught at the end of each session. The application time involved how they could take each spiritual principle and apply it to their own lives. Then they prayed for themselves, their friends, family members, fellow students, teachers, and the government and its officers. The game time encompassed an obstacle course where the kids could run through old tires, climb walls, and play a variety of simulation games. In the law enforcement time, we discussed Romans 13:1-4 and the importance of obeying the governing authorities and their laws. Different officers from a variety of agencies demonstrated some of their equipment and shared their personal testimony.

During the course of the week, there were two sisters who were always fooling around and getting into trouble. I spent much time with Emily and Emma discussing their poor behavior. I felt as if they had been forced to come and were not interested in the Lord. Each day, I shared an element of the gospel and on the last day gave an invitation to receive Christ as Savior and Lord. It was very low key, gentle, and optional. I wanted the Spirit to work in their hearts and minds and not my cleverness, intimidation, or persuasive ability. My desire was for all of them to believe that Jesus was God's Son as the Bible indicates.

Several children came forward while the girls sat silent in the back. After the program was completed, the two girls walked up to me and said that they had decided to receive Christ but were too embarrassed to come forward because of their poor behavior during the entire week. They told me how sorry they were and really did want to receive Jesus Christ as Savior and Lord. I reviewed the gospel with them right there. Then, they quietly and silently repented of their sins and affirmed their belief in Jesus as the Son of God. They received Him as only Savior of the world and then submitted their lives to Him as Lord.

Then I explained that I really wanted to discuss this great moment with their mother and ask if she would like them baptized as soon we could. Mom was delighted because she had been a Christian for quite a while but was not sure how to lead her girls to Christ. Some months after their baptism, they were forced to move away due to financial reasons. I did not hear from them for many years. Then one of the girls contacted me in her late twenties to let me know they were both still in love with their Savior and Lord and thanked me for the time I took with them. Of course, I gave the glory to God who did much of the work in their lives. Are you ready to receive Jesus Christ and be baptized?

Chapter 12

Accept God's Forgiveness

Once you receive Jesus Christ as Savior and Lord, you must accept His forgiveness of all your sins. Sometimes, we are held back because we think we are too sinful to forgive. This simply is not true. What Jesus Christ did on the cross was powerful enough to forgive any sin or sins. We merely have to accept God's forgiveness by faith with a sense of blessing and gratefulness. Here is an awe-inspiring truth: the moment you repent and receive Jesus Christ as Savior and Lord, all of your past, present, and future sins with the accompanying debt of punishment are washed away.

What does this mean? At the moment that you place your faith in Jesus, the penalty for all your sins that were paid at the cross is now appropriated to you directly. Eternal life became yours with full, complete, and total forgiveness of sin. Since this is a spiritual process, there may not have been a great feeling of relief or a tremendous sense of forgiveness at this defining moment in our lives. Instead, we should claim this forgiveness by faith.

To fully accept this forgiveness in our lives graciously and thankfully, we should understand exactly what happened at the cross. The second person of the Trinity entered humanity for the purpose of dying for man's sins. The Father punished Jesus, the God-Man, instead of us to satisfy His just and holy wrath. God has no wrath toward us for the sins we now commit toward Him or others. In Romans 4:8, Paul explains our blessed state, "Blessed is the man whom the Lord will by no means charge with sin." There is the sense of blessing and gratefulness. God, our Father, will not charge us with our sin. In Hebrews 8:12, the author speaks for God when he writes,

"For I will be merciful to their unrighteousness. I will remember their sins and lawless deeds no more."

In John 19:30, the apostle records the Christ's final words before his death, "When Jesus therefore had received the vinegar, he said, 'It is finished.' He bowed his head, and gave up his spirit." The three words translated "it is finished" is one word in the Greek meaning "to finish, complete." The word was used in secular life as a contractual term meaning "payment in full." In ancient times, someone would borrow money and sign a contract.

When the debt was fully paid, it would be stamped "Payment in Full." We will see this same phrase stamped on receipts today. The debt for our sins was fully paid on the cross. As His life was pouring out of Him, Jesus was declaring, "The penalty is now paid in full." Jesus had come to suffer and die for us, to pay all the debts of our sin and punishment, and it was completed. As soon as Jesus Christ uttered these words, He gave up His spirit to the Father. When you receive Christ, your penalty is paid. Your debt is all gone.

Paul deepens our concept of what happened on the cross in Colossians 2. In verses 13-14, Paul explained, "You were dead in your trespasses and the uncircumcision of your flesh. He made you alive together with him, having forgiven us all our trespasses, wiping out the certificate of debt which was decrees against us; and he has taken it out of the way, nailing it to the cross" (DEJ). Christ has taken the certificate of debt consisting of decrees against us and He has nailed them to the cross. What are these "decrees?" The decrees are the many judgments against us for every transgression we ever committed, are committing, or will ever commit. Our sins are written in books which Christ will open on the day of final judgment with every single, name, date, and time.

In Matthew 16:27, the Lord Jesus proclaimed, "For the Son of Man will come in the glory of his Father with his angels, and then he will render to everyone according to his deeds." The rendering He is referring to involves these specific decrees which are against us for every sin. The book of Revelation describes exactly what that judgment will entail. In Revelation 20:12, John portrays it this way, "I saw the dead, the great and the small, standing before the throne, and they opened books. Another book was opened, which is the book of life." Believers are judged from the book of life but unbelievers from the other books. John continues, "The dead were judged out of the things which were written in the books, according to their works." This would have been our fate before we placed our faith in Jesus Christ and what He did on the cross for us.

Standing before a righteous and wrathful God, we would have been judged and punished for all eternity. How many decrees against us would we have with a lifetime of sinning? More than we could possibly count! Our iniquities were paid for by our Lord Jesus Christ in his death and nailed to His cross. In Hebrews 9:22, the author of Hebrews declares in the final part of the verse, "Apart from shedding of blood there is no remission." Through the shed blood of the Lord, these sins and decrees were nailed to the cross and wiped away.

In Ephesians 1:7-8, Paul portrays what Jesus was able to accomplish, "In whom we have our redemption through his blood, the forgiveness of our trespasses, according to the riches of his grace, which he made to abound toward us in all wisdom and prudence." Notice what the apostle states concerning God's grace. The words "made to abound" is only one Greek word meaning "to exceed a fixed number of measure, to be over, abundant, excelling beyond." His grace overflowed exceedingly and beyond anything that could be measured in order to forgive. Notice it is "according to the riches of His grace." Paul did not say "out of" but "according to" the riches of His grace. This grace is infinite, knowing no bounds, which makes His forgiveness infinite and knowing no bounds. The word translated "riches" is a Greek word meaning "wealth." According to the abundant wealth of His grace came forgiveness. It came when we received Christ. So, once you receive Jesus Christ, you merely claim by faith His forgiveness of all your sins.

After I received Jesus as Savior and Lord, I went through a time of great evangelistic fervor. I wanted to share Christ and have people experience the forgiveness that I felt. I had gotten a job during the summer at an amusement park while I attended college. I began developing relationships with the many employees and witnessing for Christ. As I shared Christ with a young lady, she began to discuss what she was learning with her store manager. When she mentioned my name, Shannon, the manager, realized we had been drama club buddies in high school.

On her next break, she came looking for me. She found me in the employee's cafeteria having lunch with two others. Shannon walked up, stood in front of me, and interrupted us. Then Shannon smiled and declared, "Hey, Jones, when did you become religious?" I turned and looked at her and responded, "Six months ago when I received Christ as Savior and Lord." We grinned at each other and set a time to catch up the next day. When we got together it was like we had never been apart. We became once again close friends.

As we caught up, it was like we had chosen completely opposite paths in life. I applied to college, and she went out and got a job. While I was studying, she was partying. While I was seeking the answers to the fundamental philosophical questions of life, she was seeking the fundamental sensory pleasures of this life. One day, I walked Shannon to her car and saw a large painting of a snake on the back of it. When I asked her about it, she told me that everybody called her the "Serpent Lady." I made the casual comment, "You know one of the names of Satan in the Bible is the Serpent of Old."

She immediately made a humorous remark and changed the subject, but I knew that it bothered her. She responded by telling me she had grown up reading the Bible and knew the story of Satan tempting Adam and Eve in the garden, but she explained that she was not interested in that "religious mumbo jumbo" anymore. After this remark, Shannon and I began an ongoing, almost daily conversation about the Bible and whether it was mumbo jumbo. With every chance I got, I would share the good news of Jesus Christ with her. I tried not to be pushy or overbearing but to have a gentle, casual conversation. I cared for her and didn't want her to perish.

Then one night, a female friend of mine and I offered her a ride home. The serpent car was out of commission. As we were discussing the events of the day, she suddenly stopped. Shannon looked at me and admitted how utterly miserable she was. Though she looked outwardly like she was happy and had everything together, inwardly she felt completely empty. Shannon knew she had done some terrible things in her life and told me that God could never forgive her.

She did not want to believe in what Jesus Christ did on the cross for her and accept His forgiveness. I told her that Jesus wanted to forgive her and died for her sins. We prayed that the Holy Spirit would open her heart to these truths. Finally, after some time she said, "Yes, I finally am ready. I want to receive Jesus as Savior and Lord. I am ready to rid myself of these horrible sins and find forgiveness. In that car traveling on a freeway in Southern California, I led her in the prayer and commitment that allowed her to be forgiven and enter into eternal life. The next day, she was standing in the employee's cafeteria and called to me and said, "Hey Don, come over and talk to my friend, she feels empty like I did." She became an amazing witness for Christ at that park and in her party crowd.

Everybody she knew saw the amazing transformation in her life and everywhere she went she shared the gospel. Shannon went on to marry a pastor and live a life dedicated to the Lord Jesus. She has found the hope in this life which He provides. She had found the light to heaven and would have a happy ending. Will you? Will you receive Jesus as your Savior and accept His full forgiveness for your sins?

Chapter 13

Enjoy God's Blessings

If you decide to become a believer, then what is in it for you? That is a fair and important question. This life on Earth has a myriad of Earthly pleasures and pursuits. This is why most people reject the gospel. They do not want to give up all of it (Romans 1:18-20). I could try and soften the Bible's message as many so-called Christian's have done by telling you that you will achieve even more prosperity on this Earth if you add Jesus to your life. I could explain to you how God loves you and desires that you flourish and prosper upon His Earth in any way you desire. Just receive Jesus and like a genie in a bottle, just rub His cross, and you will get whatever you want.

This simply is not true and is not what Jesus offered when He asked people to become a part of His kingdom. Jesus did not offer prosperity but sacrifice. He did not offer physical wealth but spiritual riches. The Lord did not offer physical flourishing and prosperity; instead, He offered all spiritual blessings and an eternal inheritance.

This was to be accomplished through an exchange. You give up this life and its many sinful pursuits for Him and He will give to you His life and its many blessings. In Matthew 16:24-26, it says, "Then Jesus said to his disciples, 'If anyone desires to come after me, let him deny himself, and take up his cross, and follow me. For whoever desires to save his life will lose it, and whoever will lose his life for my sake will find it. For what will it profit a man, if he gains the whole world, and forfeits his life [soul]? Or what will a man give in exchange for his life [soul]?" Here Jesus Christ challenges His disciples (and now us) to forsake our lives and all that the world offers us in terms of money, pleasure, and power. Ultimately, this will profit us nothing! In exchange, He will give us eternal life with its many blessings and inheritance (heaven).

In this chapter, I will briefly describe the blessings that are yours if you receive Him as Savior and Lord. In the next chapter, I explain what Paul calls our heavenly inheritance. In Ephesians 1:3, Paul describes Christians as those who have been blessed with "every spiritual blessing in the heavenly places in Christ." All the blessings that God can give, He gave. I would like to explain a few of these for you.

First, our standing before God has changed. Every one of our past, present, and future sins are forgiven (Colossians 1:14; Ephesians 1:7; 4:32). Paul states that they and the debt of judgment that they brought were nailed to the cross. Then we became justified before the Almighty (Romans 5:1). This means that we were declared righteous by being given the righteousness of Christ (Romans 4:6). There is absolutely no condemnation from God (Romans 8:1, 33-34; 5:16). We are fully at peace with Him (John 14:27).

Second, our identity has changed. We become children of God (Ephesians 1:5; John 1:12). We enter a true and abiding relationship with our God as a Father (Romans 8:15). We become brothers and sisters of Jesus (Matthew 12:49), and each other (1 Peter 3:8) and are a part of a new family of God (John 1:12). In 1 Peter 2:9, Peter describes believers in this way, "But you are a chosen race, a royal priesthood, a holy nation, a people for God's own possession." We have finally found a place to belong! We are part of the family of God serving Him as chosen, royal, holy priests, possessions, and a nation. Who on Earth has a better purpose than this? Is it a president, an emperor, a prime minister, or a king? No!

Third, our being has changed. In 2 Corinthians 5:17, Paul says, "Therefore if anyone is in Christ, he is a new creation. The old things have passed away. Behold, all things have become new." The word "new" means "brand-new, new of a different kind." Our old inner person and ways of thinking, feeling, and doing become brand-new. We have a new inner person. We begin a life-long transformation into becoming Christ-like. What does this entail? Christians become fully alive spiritually (Ephesians 2:1). We are now able to think and understand the things of God (2 Corinthians 2:14).

This is accomplished through His Holy Spirit who enters our physical bodies and then takes up residence within us (Romans 8:9; 1 Corinthians 6:19). If we yield to Him by desiring to live for our God according to His Scriptures, we will experience His divine fruits. These are discussed in Galatians 5:22-23, "But the fruit of the Spirit is love, joy, peace, patience, kindness, goodness, faith, gentleness, and self-control." This is nothing like the temporal feelings that are produced by the world's fun and pleasure, or the joy and peace of drugs and alcohol. It goes so much deeper because it is divine not human.

Fourth, our bondage to sin has changed. What do I mean by this? Unbelievers are living in the domain or kingdom of darkness (Colossians 1:12-13). This domain is ruled by the prince of the power of the air who is the Devil (Ephesians 2:2). They are slaves of sin and wickedness following after the lusts of the flesh (Romans 6:6; 1 Peter 4:3). Their father is Satan himself (John 8:44) being His children (1 John 3:10). After receiving Jesus as Savior and Lord, we are transferred from the domain of darkness into the kingdom of Christ. We are now able to overcome sin and live righteously (Romans 6:14, 17-18, 22; 8:13). Of course, this will not be perfect as long as we have these old bodies that continually entice us (Romans 7:5, 24); yet, we are freed from sin's death grip.

Fifth, our fear of trials and trauma has changed. We are not shielded from all the trials that may come our way. Though God does protect His children from harm in ways that he does not for others (Romans 1:18-19; Psalm 3:3; 18:30; 115:9). We know that no matter what happens, whether it is from our own faults or others, everything will work through God's power toward our good (Romans 8:28). Trauma will come to demonstrate our faith in Christ and to push and prod us toward maturity in Him (James 1:2). During these dark moments we can rely upon His strength to endure with joy and dignity (Philippians 4:13; 2 Corinthians 12:8-10). Most of all, we will no longer fear the ultimate trial of death because it will be our doorway to the greatest blessing which is heaven itself (Hebrews 2:15; Philippians 1:19). In the midst of it all, we will always be able to go to the throne of God boldly to petition Him for whatever we may need during these difficult times (1 John 3:21-22; James 1:5).

Sixth, our relationships to others have changed. We have become an important part of the church, the Body of Christ (1 Corinthians 12:27). This church of Jesus Christ is meant to support you as you support it while you attempt to live for Him on this Earth. They become your new spiritual family (Matthew 12:49; John 1:12). As a result, we together are to love one another (John 13:34), accept one another (Romans 15:17), serve one another (Galatians 5:13), carry each other's burdens (Galatians 6:2), forgive one another (Colossians 3:16), be kind to one another (Ephesians 4:32), warn one another to keep from harm (Romans 15:14), and encourage one another (Hebrews 10:24). These ways of behaving are only a few of the numerous ways in which God's family takes care of each other. There is no organization on Earth like a fully functioning church of true Christians.

Sixth, our life goals have completely changed. We are now caught up in the greatest purpose for which people can live and that is building up the kingdom of God on Earth as we await the coming of Christ (James 5:7-8; revelation 3:11). This "building" has several aspects. The first one is the physical advancement of Jesus Christ's kingdom through sharing the gospel (Acts 1:8). The second is the spiritual growth of the church by sharing our spiritual gifts in ministry and service (1 Corinthians 12-14). The third is to raise up families who are dedicated to the Lord Jesus (Ephesians 6:4). If single, they should be devoted to the Lord (1 Corinthians 7:32). The fourth is personally growing in the Lord (1 Peter 2:2; 1 John 2:13-14). I will discuss in more detail in the second book. What other purpose could possibly be greater than continually serving the Living God? This fulfills like nothing else.

Seventh, we will find joy. Right now, you may experience the pleasure of sin such as partying, drunkenness, and other behaviors (1 John 2:16). You might be participating in the delights of the Earth such as sunsets and beaches (Psalm 4:7). You are probably involved in the "fun" of human activities such as sports and hobbies. You hopefully have found the real happiness of various relationships such as with friends, spouses, and children. The sinful pleasures won't satisfy. The other two will come and go, but Christians experience the joy of God that lasts. It is a divine joy and one that we can pursue. In Philippians 4:4, Paul says, "Rejoice in the Lord always! Again I will say, 'Rejoice!'" Here Paul commands Christians to find their joy in the Lord Jesus. We can have constant joy if we pursue Him and He's available all day, every day.

When I came to Christ as a sophomore in college, I began attending a very large church in Southern California. I joined their college ministry which was filled with very committed Christians. One night, Nick, the music leader from our bible study, was hit by a drunk driver and rushed to the hospital. The doctors were predicting that he had a 98% chance of remaining in a vegetative state for life, if he survived.

The next day, when I went to visit him, I expected to see a few people in the waiting room, and instead, experienced something that was absolutely divine. As I approached the hospital, there was a group of college students praying on the sidewalk, then others praying in the parking lot. There were groups praying in the main lobby, in the hallway to the elevator, in the waiting room, in the hallways approaching his room, in front of his room, and in his room. Everywhere we looked, students were praying. The thing that struck me the most was the calmness that had settled over them. I did not understand what this meant.

They had set up a schedule to be at the hospital 24 hours a day until God answered their prayers one way or the other. I asked if I could be a part and joined a group. The second night, I was walking out to the car with one of the leaders and asked him why everybody seemed to be so calm. He looked at me and said, "If God chooses to take him home he will have the blessings of heaven. If God chooses to keep him here, he will have the blessings of God no matter what state God decides to allow him to live in. This is all about Him and His great power and grace." I wondered what God would do and begged the Lord to give me this leader's sense of blessing.

Within days, the physicians had changed their prognosis. Within weeks, they began to talk "miracle." He not only survived but completely recovered. I knew that if God had allowed Nick to remain in that vegetative state, He would never leave his side. It was then that I realized that as Christians we are always in a "win-win" situation no matter what life brings our way. Do you want to be in that win-win situation for the rest of your life?

Chapter 14

Anticipate Your Inheritance

When you receive Jesus as Savior and Lord your eternal destiny will forever change. You will become a possessor of eternal life. You do not have to worry whether God will judge the "good" and "bads" of your life on a divine scale and then cast you into everlasting joy or fire. This is a myth. One is either a saint (holy one separated to God) or one is not (separated from God). In 1 John 5:11-12, John wrote, "He who has the Son has the life. He who doesn't have God's Son doesn't have the life. These things I have written to you who believe in the name of the Son of God that you may know that you have eternal life, and that you may continue to believe in the name of the Son of God." Those who have the Son have eternal life. It is not given at the end; it is given on the day of salvation!

This is why Paul referred to Christians often as "saints." The word "saint" means "holy one or wholly separate one." We have been separated from the world and given eternal life as possessors of the Lord Jesus Christ. Luke, the inspired writer who was the companion of Paul, in Acts 9:32 speaks of the church in Lydda as the saints. He pens, "As Peter went throughout all those parts, he came down also to the saints who lived at Lydda." Paul opens his letter to the Roman church with these words, "To all who are in Rome, beloved of God, called to be saints" (Romans 1:7). In 1 Corinthians 1:2, Paul writes, "To the assembly of God which is at Corinth; those who are sanctified in Christ Jesus, called to be saints." The author of Hebrews closes his letter with "Greet all of your leaders and all the saints. The Italians greet you" (Hebrews 13:24). Jude, the brother of Jesus describes the Scriptures as the "faith which was once for all delivered to the saints" (Jude 1:3). Every Christian is a saint now and a possessor of eternal life.

We have discussed the Earthy blessings which are a part of this eternal life, now we move on to the eternal blessings after death. This is referred to as heaven: the dwelling place of God. This is our inheritance as Christians (Ephesians 1:11) and we anticipate and look forward to it (James 5:7). This blessing has two aspects to it. The first is the privilege of living with God and His Son in His Spirit forever and ever. The second is the honor of being rewarded for the good and righteous works we have done on Earth. This would refer to any good done for the sake of Christ.

The Holy Scriptures give us only a glimpse of heaven. In several places in the Bible the curtain of mystery is pulled back, and we are afforded a dazzling display of this heavenly abode where the throne of God dwells (Isaiah 6:1; Ezekiel 1:26; Daniel 7:9). This heaven (dwelling place of God) will someday intersect with a new heavens (universe) and Earth with the throne room of God dwelling in a new holy city (Jerusalem) in between. Our heavenly abode will actually be a new Earth.

Peter describes the complete destruction of the old sin-filled heavens (universe) and Earth. In 2 Peter 3:10, Peter portrays it this way, "But the day of the Lord will come as a thief in the night; in which the heavens will pass away with a great noise, and the elements will be dissolved with fervent heat, and the Earth and the works that are in it will be burned."

Then he continues his description in verse 12-13, "Looking for and earnestly desiring the coming of the day of God, which will cause the burning heavens to be dissolved, and the elements will melt with fervent heat." Everything will be destroyed. Then he describes the new that will come, "But, according to his promise, we look for new heavens and a new Earth, in which righteousness dwells." This Greek word translated "new" means "brand-new, a new of a different kind." This "new" heaven (universe) and Earth will be suited for God's saints to dwell on forever and ever.

The apostle John was given a vision of this place we shall forever enjoy. In Revelation 21:1-4, the apostle displays its beauty in this powerful way, "I saw a new heaven and a new Earth: for the first heaven and the first Earth have passed away, and the sea is no more. I [John] saw the holy city, New Jerusalem, coming down out of heaven from God, prepared like a bride adorned for her husband. I [John] heard a loud voice out of heaven saying, 'Behold, God's dwelling is with people, and he will dwell with them, and they will be his people, and God himself will be with them as their God. He will wipe away from them every tear from their eyes. Death will be no more; neither will there be mourning, nor crying, nor pain, any more. The first things have passed away.'"

Later, he continues his powerful description in verses 23-26, "The city has no need for the sun, neither of the moon, to shine, for the very glory of God illuminated it, and its lamp is the Lamb. The nations will walk in its light. The kings of the Earth bring the glory and honor of the nations into it. Its gates will in no way be shut by day (for there will be no night there), and they shall bring the glory and the honor of the nations into it so that they may enter."

In Revelation 22:1-5, the next chapter, John describes, "He [an angel] showed me a river of water of life, clear as crystal, proceeding out of the throne of God and of the Lamb, in the middle of its street. On this side of the river and on that was the tree of life, bearing twelve kinds of fruits, yielding its fruit every month. The leaves of the tree were for the healing of the nations. There will be no curse anymore. The throne of God and of the Lamb will be in it, and his servants serve him. They will see his face, and his name will be on their foreheads. There will be no night, and they need no lamp light; for the Lord God will illuminate them. They will reign forever and ever." These are just a few of the rich scenes that have been unveiled to believers concerning their beautiful heavenly abode.

The next aspect is the reward that we will receive for our obedience to the Lord. Paul describes the reward process. In 2 Corinthians 5:10, Paul writes this, "For we must all be revealed before the judgment seat of Christ; that each one may receive the things in the body, according to what he has done, whether good or bad [not sinful but useless]." We will receive rewards for the good deeds we have done in Christ's name but not the neutral actions (hobbies, activities, sports).

Though it is difficult to know for sure all the rewards we shall obtain, we do know that it will have something to do with the robes and crowns we wear. In Revelation 19:7-8, the saints will enjoy a great feast with the Lord Jesus Christ wearing white robes. John describes it in these words, "'Let us rejoice and be exceedingly glad, and let us give the glory to him. For the marriage of the Lamb has come, and his wife has made herself ready.' It was given to her that she would array herself in bright, pure, fine linen: for the fine linen is the righteous acts of the saints." It appears that Christians will wear white robes imprinted with their righteous deeds.

The Scriptures describe various crowns we will be given. The word used refers not to the crowns kings wore but the wreaths of honor victors in athletic games wore. There are five major wreaths of honor mentioned: the incorruptible crown (1 Corinthians 9:25-27), the crown of rejoicing (Daniel 12:3; 1

Thess. 2:19-20), the crown of life (Revelation 2:10; James 1:2-3), the crown of righteousness (2 Timothy 4:8), and the crown of glory (Acts 20:26-28, 1 Pet. 5:2-4). This is just a taste of the heavenly blessings which are given to those believers who are willing to give up the life they desire to live for the life Christ desires them to live.

As a Senior Pastor, I had only been in this ministry for two years when a wonderful, Spirit-filled elderly woman in my congregation came to me with an important request. Elizabeth inquired, "Pastor, I have prayed persistently over thirty-four years for the salvation of my brother-in-law. He has lived a godless, sin-filled life of pleasure-seeking and wickedness. Now he is in the hospital dying of throat cancer. Could you possibly visit Joe and share the gospel with him? I am afraid soon it will be too late, and he will perish." So, I immediately agreed, not realizing what I was to encounter.

I asked her to pray that I would receive from the Lord an opportunity to share the good news with him and that he would see his sin and repent. A couple of days later, I entered the hospital waiting room and saw Elizabeth with another woman standing together. As I greeted them, the woman, whose name was Brenda, introduced herself as Joe's wife. She walked us out to the patio and pointed to a man sitting on a chair across the way and shouted, "Joey, Joey, Elizabeth's pastor has come by to see you, please say hello."

In front of me sat literally the shell of an eighty-five-year-old man with half of his face and lips eaten away by cancer. He was smoking a cigarette out of the other half of his lip. I was taken aback and uttered in the silence of my own soul, "Oh no, help me Lord Jesus!" He looked up, took a puff of his cigarette, gave me the once over, and then growled in a nasal tone, "I know why you're here. Well, don't bother!" In shock, I stood there. I was speechless. I began to pray for wisdom and waited for the Lord to work in some way. Then suddenly, I heard myself saying with great enthusiasm and vigor, "Well Joey, I can see this is not a good time, if I come back to see you, will you turn me away? He replied with a deep grown, "Nooooo." As I passed the two ladies saying my good-byes, I whispered, "Pray, Pray hard!"

At first, I thought to myself, I never want to see that man again. Then I remembered the role God had given me to play in His redemptive plan: Joey could not be saved if I did not share the good news with him. God would not drop a message from heaven. I was His instrument. I recommitted myself to my role in his possible salvation. I had planned on visiting him about four days later after more prayer, but on the second day, the phone rang. It was Joey's wife explaining to me that Joey wanted to see me right away. I was stunned and awestruck at God's divine sovereignty. He really was in control. I replied that I would be by the next day.

I walked into Joey's hospital room, and he motioned me to come over to him. He muttered, "Pastor, come close and talk into my right ear, it's the good one, and tell me what you have to say!" This was like a dream. It was a dream born out of thirty-four years of prayer and God's wondrous work. I began to share with him the full gospel of Jesus Christ. As I talked about sin and judgment, I prayed God would convict Him through His Holy Spirit.

Joey sat there for a good thirty minutes, never saying a word, only quietly listening and weeping. Sometimes, I had to shout over his sobbing. When I got to the end, my heart was pounding in my chest, and I boldly asked, "Well, would you like to become a Christian? And Joey shook his head and whimpered, "Yeeeeesss." As we prayed together, I asked Joey to silently describe to the Lord some of the sins he had committed and admit them to Him. Then, he needed to tell

Him how sorry he was and that he would turn from them in the little time he may have left on this Earth. He did.

After this he received Jesus as His Savior and Lord and became a Christian. Then, he begged me to baptize him even though he knew he would never get out of that bed again. I called his brother and sister-in-law to come to the hospital room and his nurse. Right there, I poured a little water over his head as Joey shared his testimony with them. Normally, I would immerse Him in the water as is always seen in the New Testament, but he would not have survived that.

Every visit Joey would tell me how he had talked to a nurse or doctor about the Lord. He said he didn't have much time, but he wanted some of that reward Paul talked about. Then he would ask me to tell him all about the heaven and eternal life he had now possessed. Tears of joy were always in his eyes as he asked question after question about his new eternity. Three weeks later, I went to enjoy some fellowship with him, and his bed was empty. Joey had passed away and into the arms of His Savior and Lord. He spent his last days anticipating his inheritance. Would you like the inheritance of heaven and reward?

FINDING THE LIGHT

Chapter 15

Live for Christ First

Before you receive Christ, it is important for you to know exactly what you are getting yourself into. Jesus called it "counting the cost." In Luke 14:26-27, Jesus discusses the cost of becoming one of His followers. Your loyalty must change from whatever it is to Christ first. This does not mean you go off into the desert and live like a monk, but it does mean that the Lord has expectations for you and me as we live in His kingdom on Earth. The death of Jesus on the cross is not a free ticket to live anyway we like. At the end, we can take it out and hand it to the Lord as entrance into His kingdom. Instead, it is a supernatural ticket to a journey of honoring and glorifying Him which begins at the moment of salvation and continues into eternity.

The Lord compares counting the cost of membership in His kingdom to a king going out to battle and a builder building a tower. He uses two analogies in this counting the cost discussion. In Luke 14:28-30, the Lord describes the builder, "For which of you, desiring to build a tower, doesn't first sit down and count the cost, to see if he has enough to complete it? Or perhaps, when he has laid a foundation, and is not able to finish, everyone who sees begins to mock him, saying, 'This man began to build, and wasn't able to finish.'" Here is someone who doesn't have enough materials or the motivation for completing the tower and abandons it.

In Luke 14:31-32, Jesus presents His second analogy, "Or what king, as he goes to encounter another king in war, will not sit down first and consider whether he is able with ten thousand to meet him who comes against him with twenty thousand? Or else, while the other is yet a great way off, he sends an envoy, and asks for conditions of peace." Here a king goes out to battle without considering carefully the sacrifices he may have to make. This results in the surrender of his army.

These are the people who come to Christ out of emotion or some inspirational or motivational speech. They do not consider the commitment that must be made, the new life that must be lived, maybe even the persecution that must be endured. Sometimes people do not know because the one sharing with them did not tell them. This is why I am telling you. I know this sounds a bit stoic, but the commitment will come from the joy and power of the Holy Spirit which will indwell you. Why wouldn't we desire to obey the Lord who has given us so much?

In Philippians 2:12-13, Paul explains that believers are to work out their salvation as God is at work in them to do His will. This does not refer to doing good works to be saved. It refers to working out all the aspects of our salvation toward one important end which is our lifelong transformation into the likeness of Jesus Christ. God desires for His children to think, speak, and act like His Son in their lives on this Earth. This is called spiritual growth.

As we live our Christian lives, we are to grow into the image of Christ. In Ephesians 4:13, Paul describes the goal of the church on Earth as attaining to the unity of the faith and of the knowledge of the Son. We do this both individually and corporately until we become full grown and mature in Christ. This means we are to measure up to the "stature of the fullness of Christ." This would be like a brother standing next to his older brother attempting to grow into his image. We are standing next to Jesus and growing into his spiritual image checking our character, attitudes, and lifestyle.

What does this mean? It simply means that if Christ was dependent on God, then we learn to be dependent on God. If Christ was patient, we learn to be patient. If Christ obeyed God's commands, we learn to obey God's commands. This spiritual growth process into the image of Christ consists of scriptural study, intercessory prayer, fellowship with the saints, sound instruction, ministering one's gifts, sharing the gospel, living righteously, and enduring trials.

Let's take each of these briefly. If you become a believer, God desires that you read His Bible regularly. Why? This is how He speaks to His people. When we are in a relationship with someone, would it be a good idea to never allow them to speak to us or to refuse to hear anything they had to say? If we had a boss who we worked for, would it be a brilliant idea if we never asked what He wanted us to do or read his training manual for the job? Both of the answers are obvious. We need to allow the Lord to speak to us in His Word.

So, believers need a consistent time of study in the Bible. It is the Word of God that the Holy Spirit uses to transform you into Christ's image. In 1 Thessalonians 2:13, the apostle Paul explains how the Bible works, "For this cause, we also thank God without ceasing, that, when you received from us the word of the message of God, you accepted it not as the word of men, but, as it is in truth, the word of God, which also works in you who believe."

This work that God's Word performs in our lives is the changing of our old unrighteous thoughts and ways to God's righteous thoughts and ways. The Lord God requires us to live supernaturally upon this Earth, not naturally (man's way). The Lord sometimes asks us to think and behave in ways that seem contrary to everything we hold true, such as the loving of our enemies (Matthew 5:44) or forgiving people over and over again (Matthew 18:22).

115

In a relationship, not only are we to allow God to talk to us, but we are to talk to Him. This is called prayer. In 1 John 5:14, the apostle John describes prayer as boldly being in the presence of God face to face and communicating with Him. In many of Paul's letters, he asks for prayer (Colossians 4:3-5) and requests that the saints pray for others (Ephesians 6:18). In fact, in 1 Thessalonians 5:17, the apostle encourages Christians to never stop praying. Praying is a critical part of the Christian life and assists us in our spiritual growth.

The third kind of divine living is to "fellowship" with other believers. The apostle John uses this word to describe the interaction of the saints. In 1 John 1:6-7, he speaks of our "fellowship" with one another. The Greek word connotes a "joint participation" in something. We are involved in a joint participation in the advancement of the Kingdom of God and the spiritual maturing of the saints. The primary way we do this with believers is to interact with one another (using our giftedness) to encourage others to grow toward spiritual maturity in Christ. Also, we come along and support one another in whatever need they may have or crisis they may be going through. This would mean you would join a local Bible-believing church.

Next, we need to be taught the truths in the Scriptures. This is called teaching "sound doctrine." God has placed within the church pastor-teachers who instruct the saints in sound doctrine to equip them to serve the saints in the church. In Ephesians 4:11-12, Paul describes this important principle, "He gave some to be apostles; and some, prophets; [these saints laid the foundation and have now gone] and some, evangelists and some, shepherds and teachers. For the perfecting of the saints, to the work of serving [in different ways], to the building up of the body of Christ." Paul uses two words to describe only one person who shepherds by teaching the Bible to the members of a local church.

Personal study of the Bible is good, but a strong teacher of the Word can provide the much deeper and broader truths of Scripture and their powerful applications to individual lives. The deeper truth is crucial. This is why in 1 John 2:13-14, John calls the mature Christians "spiritual fathers." Why? These mature saints know "Him who is from the beginning." Spiritual fathers so understand the Word of God that they now truly know the Son of God described in the Word. This is not done through intellectual reasoning about their faith or some divine infusion of mystical knowledge; instead, it is accomplished through a diligent and deep study of God's speaking and acting in His Word. These truths are what is taught regularly by a pastor-teacher.

The next aspect of Christian living is truly exciting. When we received Christ as Savior and Lord, every believer is given at least one spiritual gift (ability) for the good of the church and world. These gifts may or may not be tied to one's physical skills, abilities, or personality. Gifts are given to every believer by the Spirit according to God's divine will. In 1 Corinthians 12:4-7, the apostle discusses these gifts or spiritual abilities, "Now there are various kinds of gifts, but the same Spirit."

"There are various kinds of service, and the same Lord. There are various kinds of workings, but the same God, who works all things in all. But to each one [a believer] is given the manifestation of the Spirit for the profit of all." A variety of gifts are given for a variety of ministries having a variety of effects. God provides each person with a gift(s) to serve others. As we grow spiritually, read the Bible, and receive guidance from the church, we will discover and use them. This is such an important aspect of the Christian life.

Another aspect of the Christian life is what I am doing with you and that is sharing the gospel. In Acts 1:8, Jesus left the disciples and us with these words, "But you will receive power when the Holy Spirit has come upon you. You will be witnesses to me in Jerusalem, in all Judea and Samaria, and to the uttermost parts of the Earth." When the persecution of Saul erupted in its full force, the Christians were scattered. What did they do? In Acts 8:4, Luke describes it, "Therefore those who were scattered abroad went around preaching the word." This primarily speaks of verbally sharing the gospel.

Here is where the evangelist comes in; he will train us to share our true faith with others. In Matthew 5:14-16, Jesus describes how God's kingdom people act, "You are the light of the world. A city located on a hill can't be hidden." He portrays us as a lighted city on a hill for all to see. Then He asserts, "Neither do you light a lamp, and put it under a measuring basket, but on a stand; and it shines to all who are in the house." We cannot allow ourselves to cover up our lights through sinful behavior. Instead, He demands, "Even so, let your light shine before men; that they may see your good works, and glorify your Father who is in heaven."

Another aspect of being in the kingdom of God is living righteously. In 1 John 2:6, the apostle writes, "He who says he remains in him [a believer] ought himself also to walk just like he [Jesus] walked." In Colossians 1:10, Paul describes our Christian lives in this important way, "So that you will walk in a manner worthy of the Lord, to please Him in all respects, bearing fruit in every good work and increasing in the knowledge of God." We should walk about in our lives moment by moment in a manner that is worthy of the Lord. We are to live to please Him in every area of our lives (in all respects). We are to bear fruits through doing good works and increase in our knowledge of Him. How do we do this? We deepen our love of Jesus Christ and as we do we desire to obey His commandments. In 2 John 1:6, John writes these words, "This is love, that we should walk according to his commandments." In Philippians 4:9, the apostle asserts, "The things you have learned and received and heard and seen in me, practice these things, and the God of peace will be with you." It takes practice to live righteously. This kind of living is not automatic and requires supernatural strength from the Holy Spirit. As long as we have this body, we will not be able to be perfect. Instead, God desires that we grow to become more and more righteous.

Lastly, no matter how much we desire not to sin, we will. As a result, we must be prepared to stumble, fall, confess, and begin the walk again. This may occur many times a day at first, but as we grow in Christ it decreases. True believers are constantly recognizing the sins that they are committing and asking God for forgiveness. This is not just an eternal issue but also a relational one. When we received Christ as Savior and Lord, all our sins were forgiven from the past, present, and future (Colossians 2:13-14; Romans 8:1). In our relationship with God upon this Earth in the flesh, we still confess our sins. This restores our relationship with God in a relationship sense. It will eliminate any barriers between us and God.

Some were saying in the churches that they had matured to such a level that they no longer sinned in any way. John, the apostle, counters with a scathing response. In 1 John 1:8, the apostle emphatically states, "If we say that we have no sin, we deceive ourselves, and the truth is not in us." Then in verse 10, he declares, "If we say that we haven't sinned, we make him a liar, and his word is not in us." Those who were claiming that they had never sinned or no longer sinned were deceiving themselves, others, and even attempting to deceive God. Therefore, it was obvious that His truth was not in them. Why? The truth that is written in the Bible convicts believers of their sins. This sense of conviction is the evidence of the truth in them.

Then sandwiched between these two convicting passages is what believers do when they realize they have sinned. In verse 9, he proclaims, "If we confess our sins, He is faithful and righteous to forgive us the sins, and to cleanse us from all unrighteousness." The verbs "confess" and "forgive" are in the present tense which indicates continual action in present time. Believers are continually confessing their sins and God is continually forgiving them. Repentance and asking God to forgive us is a lifelong practice. This admission of sin is the first step in the confession process. In 1 John 1:9, the Greek word translated "confess" means "to say the same thing" which indicates that we are to say the same thing about our sin that God says. We tell the Lord what we did was sinful and ask for His forgiveness which He always grants.

When I was a pastor, one Sunday morning a couple with four small children came to our church. They were so taken with the preaching of God's Word (all Him, not me) that they wanted to become members within weeks. I did not know whether they had received Jesus as Savior and Lord so I asked if I could come over and talk to them. When I arrived at Eric and Tonya's house, we chatted for several minutes about various subjects. Then, I asked, "So how did you both receive Jesus Christ as Savior and Lord?" The wife went first and explained that she had grown up in a large church and had always believed in Jesus Christ from the time she was small. He claimed the exact same thing.

In fact, they had met in the church's youth group but admitted that they had not been practicing their religion for quite a while and wanted to get back to it, especially for the kids. They both told me that children should be raised with moral values. They thought, "What better place than in a church?" For some, this may have been enough, but I wanted to probe deeper. I asked them if there was ever a moment in time when they actually remember someone who shared the good news with them, being convicted of their sins, and repenting before the Lord Jesus. I inquired as to whether they had ever remembered declaring to the Father that they knew Jesus was His only Son, that He died on the cross for their sins, and asked Him to save them? I questioned them as to whether they had ever remembered a time when they submitted their lives to Christ as Lord and promised to obey Him with all their hearts? Suddenly, they both looked at me in complete bewilderment. Almost in unison, they muttered, "No, I haven't." Eric looked at me and said, "I have never done any of those things, I thought you just needed to be a member of a church to be a Christian." Tonya agreed.

I gently explained that they may have known about Jesus Christ like we know about a great historical figure. We admire the person, want to follow his values and teachings, even be like him in some ways. Yet, they do not have a living relationship with the person. Jesus Christ desires a love relationship with them. They looked puzzled because they had never even considered this. I then shared the true gospel that I have shared with you. I explained that they must receive Jesus Christ as Savior and place their lives in His hands as Lord.

After this, I inquired, "Eric and Tonya, would you want to receive Jesus Christ as Savior and Lord right now? This means that you both would enter into a real and abiding love relationship with Him by faith and enter the kingdom of heaven." They both responded, "Yes!" After coming to Christ, the very next Sunday they were baptized. Then I personally began meeting with them one evening a week. We studied the basics of the Christian life. I used a simple fill-in series of books that taught the things I have mentioned in this chapter which can be purchased at any Christian bookstore. We discussed the importance of faith over any feelings they may have. They learned that the Christian life was a walk of faith.

This life also involved a consistent time in the Scriptures, intercessory prayer, fellowshipping with other Christians, discovering their many gifts, and serving in ministry.

They must pursue righteousness as they confess their sins daily. They had found a church that taught sound doctrine, and they should attend regularly. We studied these truths together. Slowly over a period of time, they began to change their desires and their attitudes about some of the things that they were involved in that did not honor God. They found a new purpose for living and relished in the things of the kingdom of heaven. Will you receive Christ as Savior and Lord and begin this momentous journey?

Conclusion

We come to the end of this gospel presentation. You now have all that you need to receive and enter God's heaven or reject Him and continue in condemnation. I only ask that you take some time to really consider these truths. If and when you desire to receive Him, you can pray this prayer:

Dear God,

> *I want to be a part of your Son's kingdom. I know that all I deserve is judgment for my sin. I am so sorry for what I have done. I believe Jesus is your Son. I know this because he resurrected from the dead. I believe that He died on the cross to pay the penalty for my sin. I believe that He is the only way to heaven. I welcome and receive Him into my life right now as Savior. I turn my life over to Him as Lord and Master. I want a love relationship with Jesus Christ. I thank you for the blessings you are bestowing on me right now. I am grateful for my entrance into heaven which was gained by the faith your Spirit gave me and not by any works. I will do my best to live for you and fulfill the purpose for which I have been created.*

If you prayed that prayer and meant it, then the Holy Spirit has entered you; you are now a child of our God. You must find yourself a bible teaching church and begin your adventure. I would suggest you get a copy of the Bible and begin reading the Gospel of John. If this is too difficult to understand at first, then get a copy of the Living Bible. This is a paraphrase and not literal, but it will get you started.

If you choose to take some time to consider these truths, then read through the book again and look up the passages.

You may also simply read the gospel of John. It is all there. If you decide to reject Jesus Christ, please do not throw this book away. Give it back to the person who gave it to you or leave it on a table somewhere so someone else may pick it up. God will always be waiting even until the day of your death. Please be warned that once death comes, then comes judgment. In Hebrews 9:27, the author warns all of us, "In as much as it is appointed for men to die once, and after this, judgment." I leave you with the most well-known verse in the world. It is John 3:16, "For God so loved the world, that he gave his one and only Son, that whoever believes in him should not perish, but have eternal life." I hope I will see you in heaven!

ABOUT THE AUTHOR

Dr. Donald Jones is currently a Christian Pastoral Counselor with thirty-eight years of experience in the fields of pastoral ministry, public education, and Christian counseling. He carries degrees and certificates from four major universities and from a variety of educational institutions. He has been a professor of Languages and Bible, a television commentator, and a featured speaker at a variety of events and seminars at churches, schools, and other organizations across the United States. He is a member in good standing of several secular and Christian professional organizations. Dr. Jones has been a published author since 1976. For further information view his website at www.donjonesphd.com.